Praise for IAN TYSON

"Ian Tyson is the real deal. What others have imagined, Ian has lived. From a rodeo-riding youth to a broken-hearted gentleman and a prairie poet. . . . He's a romantic and a realist, a rancher and a true singing cowboy . . . he's the one Gene Autry only wished he could have been."

The San Diego Troubadour

"Tyson is hands-down the premier writer and performer of music of and about the people of the West."

Western Horseman

"Tyson's music will surely stand beside the works of his heroes as enduring documents of the West."

Los Angeles Times

"Engaging. There's no doubt Tyson has earned a place in music history."

Quill & Quire

"Tyson has had a long, fulfillingand interesting life. . . . He has become a tireless advocate for the protection of the western environment."

The Globe and Mail

The
LONG TRAIL

My Life in the West

IAN
TYSON

with Jeremy Klaszus

Vintage Canada

VINTAGE CANADA EDITION, 2011

Copyright © 2010 Four Strong Winds

Published in Canada by Vintage Canada, a division of Penguin Random House
Canada Limited, Toronto, in 2011. Originally published in hardcover in Canada by
Random House Canada, a division of Penguin Random House Canada Limited,
Toronto, in 2010. Distributed by Penguin Random House Canada Limited, Toronto.

Vintage Canada with colophon is a registered trademark.

www.penguinrandomhouse.ca

Lyrics reprinted by permission of Ian Tyson and Slick Fork Music.

Photos on pp. ii, iii, 148 and 187 reprinted by permission of Todd Korol.

Library and Archives Canada Cataloguing in Publication
data is available upon request.

Cover and text design by Terri Nimmo
Cover image: Kurt Markus

Printed in the United States of America

Penguin
Random House
VINTAGE CANADA

CONTENTS

1.   Sunrise 1

2.   West of the West 9

3.   Drifting.................... 31

4.   New York................... 52

5.   Horses..................... 73

6.   Sagebrush Renaissance 96

7.   Cowboyography 117

8.   The Changing West.......... 132

9.   Beef, Beans and Bullshit...... 149

10.   Raven Rock 175

11.   Closing the Circle............ 193

CONTENTS

CHAPTER 1

Sunrise

It's darker than three feet down a Holstein. Six a.m., Alberta daylight savings. Waking from a dream of Cabo San Lucas to a March north wind and five below. Everyone with half a brain and a Visa card has gotten out. Only us drones left to feed the livestock, so I make the coffee double strength and prepare to get at 'er. Fifteen minutes stumbling around on frozen manure should do it.

So begins the day.

Used to be a rancher wouldn't divulge the size of his operation, nor the numbers of his herd. It's a longstanding tradition in cow country that's based on making as little information available to the tax people as possible. Suffice it to say, my outfit is a modest spread near the southern Alberta town of Longview, just east of the Rocky Mountain foothills.

During the ranch's heyday in the 1990s, I ran between twenty and thirty horses. They were mostly mares, which meant there were lots of babies each year. That was back when my ex-wife Twylla and my daughter Adelita were still

On Pokey at the ranch. (LEE GUNDERSON)

here. But they left a few years back, and these days it's just me on the ranch — and only five horses to feed. There's Bud, my cutting horse, a solid professional cowhorse, all business all the time. Then there's Pokey, a bay mare, with all her feminine wiles, who loves to be the centre of attention. Every morning they're lined up for their grain.

I feed my gentle grey mare and her half-broke daughter. The mare ran under the name Lika Pop back in her race-track days and won her maiden at 350 yards. She's eighteen now and crippled with a bad knee, but she's been a good colt producer. Her daughter Doris is a big, pushy adolescent who's never been properly schooled because I don't have the time to do it. Finally there's a new colt, a trim, good-moving two-year-old. He's a blank canvas.

As for my two big longhorns, Kramer is laid back and Billy is more snuffy. While I pour their crushed barley into the rubber feed tub, their great horns sway slowly around my head in the darkness. I'm damn careful because I never know what Billy's going to do. I bought Kramer and seven other yearling bulls in the mid-1990s from the late Mitford Beard, who ran one of the last American open-range outfits (no fences) on the Utah-Colorado line. Billy came a few years later, from rancher Bill Cross.

Billy and Kramer are my last two steers, and when it's warm enough, they'll wander out of their lot onto the prairie like a couple of old outlaws. Longhorns are like pets for ranchers, reminders of a bygone era when the trail herders drove cattle across the unfenced West. They're almost conversation pieces nowadays.

Kramer sure gave me something to talk about when he got his horns stuck in a round-bale feeder a few years back.

I heard all this banging coming from his pen, and when I went up to see what was going on, there was Kramer waving around this 200-pound bale feeder like a damn party hat, repeatedly crashing it into the fence. Those feeders aren't small. They're five feet across, with diagonal steel struts around the sides above the base. I guess he'd stuck his head and horns between the struts, right inside the feeder — he was more than happy to get closer to the hay. But when he wanted to get out, he couldn't. Then the wreck was on.

I didn't know what the hell to do. I called my neighbour Pete Wambeke, and he didn't know what to do either. I couldn't rope Kramer, because he's too big and a horse couldn't hold him. I considered getting some tranquilizers from the vet, but then I thought, *I'm gonna take care of this myself.* I got my hacksaw and approached Kramer warily, talking to him for almost half an hour before he finally let me stand beside him and start sawing away at the struts to free his horns.

I knew Kramer had only so much patience and then he'd lose it again and start waving his party hat around — he was already stepping on my feet. But he's intelligent, and I guess he understood that I was going to get him out. I kept sawing, sweating like crazy. "Christ," I muttered. "If I don't have a cardiac arrest, it's going to be a miracle." Finally I got two struts cut and out he came, horns and all. He wandered off, thankful for his freedom.

Then the silly son of a bitch did the exact same thing the following year, and again I had to cut him free. After that I carefully eliminated all round-bale feeders from the long-horns' pens.

—

After feeding the horses and longhorns in the early-morning dark, I give a few leftover wieners to the kitty-cats in the barn and head back inside for breakfast. I live in a cedar-log house built in 1975. That's a big reason why I bought this land in 1979, when I was forty-six — I liked the rustic feel, as well as the huge basement. (The romance fades, however, when you realize that logs are great dust-catchers.) I also liked the big living room with its west-facing windows looking out on the shining mountains.

Today both the main floor and the basement are decorated with Navajo rugs, Mexican tile, eagle feathers, Indian artifacts and the western paintings, photos and horse sculptures I've collected over the years. In the kitchen hangs a framed poster from the inaugural 1961 Mariposa Folk Festival — a poster I designed — and there's a brand new dishwasher, my pride and joy.

I'm a bacon freak, so I fry up some bacon, boil a couple of eggs and have a grapefruit before taking my vitamin pills. I also have to take naproxen and hyaluronic acid for my hands and wrists — old cowboys have lots of aches and pains, and I've been dealing with arthritis for the past twenty years. I keep my fingers limber by practising the guitar for at least an hour a day; otherwise my hands might shut down entirely.

Guitar practice is a daily discipline for me. I never was a night writer, never could pull a Hank Williams and stay up all night drinking whiskey and writing songs. In my world, mornings are for music and afternoons are spent doing the many chores that ranches require — moving hay bales, picking up feed in nearby Okotoks and making runs to the post office.

The only way to get any real writing done in the morning, though, is to get out of the home place and away from the phones. So after breakfast, at around 8 a.m., I pull on my hiking boots and begin the walk south down the gravel road to my stone house, where I do my songwriting.

On days like this one, towards the end of winter, the sun is often late rising above the clouds banked over the eastern plains. There's no wind. The only sound is the faint humming of the power lines along the road, until the silence is broken by a raven calling as he heads for the mountains, and the distant burble of my neighbour's truck with its busted muffler.

To the right is my hayfield, a great swath of buckskin grass delineated by thin snowdrifts along the fencelines. It was dry barley land when I first came here thirty years ago, and the black soil from that field blew like crazy. But when the rains came again, we seeded it all back to top-of-the-line grassland — the kind we need more of in this country. I've formed a loose partnership with my neighbour Pete to run grass yearlings from his outfit, the Diamond V, on the hayfield in May, and this summer will be no different.

Beyond the hayfield and high above the rolling foothills, the Rockies stay shrouded in grey until the sun's first rays bathe the snow-covered peaks in rose pink and the timber foothills below in deep purple, a scene almost too theatrical to be real. I've seen the sunrise here a thousand times and it still moves me.

I arrive at the stone house after twenty minutes of walking. Built sometime in the 1920s, it has a green tin roof and sits on a wind-blasted little hill. The walls are sixteen inches thick. Originally I thought of it as a bunkhouse for itinerate punchers, but it soon became far more valuable as a music house. Now all my demos are done here — band rehearsals too. Guitars sound quite fine in the stone house in the morning, and lyrics are often found there soon after sunrise.

Before I enter, I walk to a treed area farther down the hill, where there's a group of tilting shacks that comprised the original homestead on this land. Those first homesteaders ran sheep. I knocked most of the shacks down a few years back but kept a few for the animals, and I like to see who's around in the morning. Owls keep a nest in the nearby willows, and deer sometimes yard up down there — it's great hideaway country for them when the poplars leaf out. The occasional elk wanders in, and once I even saw a big old black bear nosing around the place, a rare sight on the bald prairie.

After visiting the animals — if the neighbour's dog hasn't scared them all away — I head into the stone house. Inside I've got a few couches, a couple of old rugs spread over hardwood floors and a big wooden table for writing. I make myself another coffee in the kitchen before getting out my guitar and running the scales, doing my best to warm up my stiff fingers. I slide a Mark Knopfler CD into my stereo system — I consider him my songwriting and guitar mentor, along with Ry Cooder — and try to keep up with him for a while before tackling my own material.

It's been a long trail that brought me here. It all started September 25, 1933, on Vancouver Island — "west of the West," as my friend, the photographer Jay Dusard, put it — where I grew up in the Oak Bay area of Victoria with my mom, dad and older sister, Jean. But my earliest childhood memories are mostly lost, thanks to too many miles and too many whiskey bottles. Too many years of trying to figure out who I was — and who I wanted to become.

CHAPTER 2

West of the West

I've always wanted to be where the sagebrush grows. When he was in his late teens, my old man, George Dawson Tyson, had that same desire. He'd been born July 4, 1889, into a large Victorian upper-middle-class family a few miles west of Liverpool, in the little seaside town of Hoylake, England. Somehow he got infused with the romance of the North American West — probably by reading about Buffalo Bill's buffalo-hunting adventures — and he immigrated to Alberta in 1906 with dreams of becoming a cowboy. George arrived on the Canadian prairie green as a gourd, landing work as a ranch hand near Bowden, about sixty-five miles north of Calgary. He later told me he'd go to social events and almost freeze to death on the way back to the ranch, shivering under his buffalo robe.

The winter of 1906–07 in particular was a killer on the northern plains. Entire herds of cattle died. "The year of the blue snow" is how Wallace Stegner described it in *Wolf Willow*: "That winter has remained ever since, in the minds

My father, George Dawson Tyson, in Alberta. (COURTESY IAN TYSON)

of all who went through it, as the true measure of catastrophe." My dad had gone to Alberta seeking the romance of cowboy life, not frostbite, and after a couple of harsh winters disabused him of his puncher plans, he drifted to the more moderate climate of the West Coast. Years later he told me he'd witnessed the last of open-range ranching in Alberta.

By his telling, he also saw the last of the real Native coastal villages in the Pacific Northwest — complete with totem poles — while working for a government survey crew on Nootka Island around 1910. After that job ended, he applied for a 160-acre homestead in the bush on Vancouver Island near Cowichan Bay. He liked to tell the story of felling a bunch of arbutus trees on that homestead and dropping them into the saltchuck, where, to his surprise, all the logs promptly sank. He had to dig a well and build a rudimentary shack to improve the homestead so he could keep it, but he never got it done; the land must have reverted back to the government.

He hung out for a time with a bunch of English rounders on the island, and then the war came. In 1914 he enlisted with the Victoria-based 50th Regiment (Gordon Highlanders), which provided troops for the Canadian Expeditionary Force. My old man headed to France in April 1915 as a twenty-five-year-old private. (Many of the other CEF troops were British-born too.) Eventually he ended up as a captain in the King's Liverpool Regiment of the British Army.

I don't know all the details of his war service, but at some point — I don't know when or how — the Germans wounded him pretty severely in his neck and back. Shrapnel wounds, I suspect. After that the Germans captured him and kept him in a prisoner-of-war camp hospital for a few months. I do know that he struggled to communicate during that time because he couldn't pick up German. Eventually he was repatriated to England, where he spent some more time in hospital recovering from his war wounds. For the rest of his life he always stood a little crooked because of his neck injury.

My father said that when he got back to Duncan, B.C., after the war (that's where he lived at the time), a cenotaph had been built to commemorate the dead. His was one of the few names of young men from the area that wasn't on it. They were all killed in the early part of the war, those Canadian boys. My dad was lucky.

The British Army gave him a Military Cross, with bar — the equivalent of a second MC. The citation said the medal had been awarded for "conspicuous gallantry and devotion to duty. After ably leading his company in a successful attack on the enemy's lines, he advanced with his own and another company, filled a dangerous gap in our line and by excellent control firmly held his own against a counter attack in the face of very heavy shelling. Throughout the operation he displayed the utmost ability and skill, and kept his men's spirits up by continually pressing along the line at imminent personal risk during heavy hostile shell fire."

When I was growing up, each November my dad and I would ride our horses through the meadows and oak trees of the Uplands, an area in Oak Bay dotted with English-style estates, on what he called Armistice Day. At 11 a.m. we would dismount and stand silently for three minutes. Afterwards he would tell me some of his battle memories, recalling the rats in the trenches and the snipers that had fired upon the Allied lines. He'd also talk about the Christmastime ceasefires with the Germans, when the snipers stopped shooting for a day. The next day they'd be right back at it, killing each other again.

It's amazing that the war didn't destroy my old man the way it wrecked so many World War I vets. He saw lots of action but, for whatever reason, he didn't internalize the experience. It probably helped that he never went through a gas attack. Growing up on Vancouver Island, I saw many of those old English guys who'd been gassed in the war, and a lot of them were crazy.

After the war, George met my mother, Margaret Gertrude Campbell, a native-born islander with a Scots Presbyterian background. (Her people had come to Victoria from Ontario — probably via San Francisco — in the 1870s, and her father, Duncan Campbell, ran a successful apothecary.) My mom's parents owned a summer home at Cadboro Bay, just east of the present-day University of Victoria, and my dad often stayed at the nearby Cadboro Bay Hotel. Somehow my mom and dad met on the beach, and they married on June 18, 1930. He was thirty-nine; she was twenty-six.

Their first child, Jean Tyson, was born the following year. Jean was always a shy kid. After I was born, in 1933, she felt I got all the attention from our parents, and she was probably right. We didn't like each other very much as kids and we squabbled constantly, especially when we played Monopoly.

It sounds strange, but I never really knew my mother. She wasn't an extrovert by any means — she kept her thoughts and feelings pretty much to herself. She had four siblings, a couple of whom were alcoholics, and as a result my mom didn't drink. Unlike my dad, she was pretty severe; she didn't approve of "loose morals" at all. She was always there for me over the years, but poor Mother lived a pretty dour life.

She had fully bought into Presbyterian doctrine, and at Christmas and Easter she'd drag Jean and me to St. Andrew's Presbyterian Church, a big brick building on the corner of Douglas and Broughton streets in downtown Victoria. I hated going there and really disliked the music — it was terrible. That poor organ at St. Andrew's suffered great musical indignities in the cause of Presbyterianism. I would have much preferred it if Mother had hauled us to a Baptist or Pentecostal church, where the music was more rockin.'

The first house Jean and I lived in was a bungalow on Dufferin Avenue, just west of Cattle Point. Our house was surrounded by big open fields, little oak trees and scotch broom — beautiful country, almost like range. The green meadows stretched right down to the ocean. It felt like we were out in the country, yet the Uplands just north of our place was furnished with paved roads connecting the houses, lit by ornate cast iron lampposts just like you'd find in a city. It was a lovely arrangement, and I don't think I've seen anything like it since. That entire area is now completely developed, but back then the suburbanization of Victoria, a civil-service town of old brick and wooden buildings, was only just beginning.

People living there when I was a kid liked to pretend they were British; they thought of their city as a bastion of the British Empire, strong and loyal. My earliest memory is of bonfires burning all along the rocky coastline of Cattle Point in 1939 as people eagerly awaited the arrival of King George VI and Queen Elizabeth, whose steamship was to come up the coast and into Victoria Harbour. There the royal party would mingle with their loyal subjects. I was five at the time, and I seem to remember people waving little Union Jacks as they waited for the ocean liner, a surreal scene that plays like an old movie in my mind.

In addition to the anglophile culture, a whole other class of people thrived on the island. Immigrants — Danes, Swedes, Norwegians, Irish — drove the economy, working as loggers, fishermen and miners. And as you went north up Vancouver Island, the pretensions of mock empire rapidly gave way to a working-class ethic that attracted me even as a little boy. Those guys were out in the fresh air doing hard labour, and it seemed like a lot more fun than working in a stuffy downtown office as a civil servant. Of course, as a kid I didn't realize just how hard their manual labour was.

Even in the depths of the Great Depression, the feeling on Vancouver Island was one of optimism. There would never be an end to the big timber. The salmon and other fishing stocks were inexhaustible. The natural resources would last forever. A strong man would always find work. This was not the Dust Bowl.

My old man managed the Monarch Life Assurance Company's Victoria branch, which sold life insurance to loggers. That wasn't a bad idea, since those guys were always getting killed in spectacular accidents. He'd go up the coast on a little steamer to Port Alberni and Port Renfrew to do business. When he was home, he was always busy, a hyper banty rooster of a man. He wasn't that big — five foot eight — and had black hair very much in the style of the 1930s, like British-American actor Cary Grant's. He was very proud of his hair.

When Jean and I were really young, Dad used to take us up to Smugglers Cove, on Ten Mile Point, a peninsula that sticks out into the Strait of Juan de Fuca. We'd all stand on the rocks and watch the killer whales going north in their spring migration as seabirds wheeled overhead. The old man would bring along some glittery jewellery he had bought at Woolworth's, which he'd bury in the sand. Then he'd tell Jean and me that if we dug deep enough we might find treasure. That memory has stayed with me; I wrote a song about it ("Smugglers Cove") more than six decades later:

Father took me by the hand
Down through the rocks and driftwood
And pirate gold from the five and dime
He caused me to discover
All in a morning's wonder

The old man never came to church with Mom, Jean and me. His church was the great outdoors.

We're pretty similar, the old man and I. He approached life in a very visceral, non-intellectual way, always living in the moment and having fun. He loved fishing and riding horses, though he wasn't very good at either. He was certainly no horseman. I haven't a clue how he got into horses — he might have learned when he went to boarding school on the Isle of Man, in the Irish Sea — but his idea of riding was simply to hop on and go fast. He didn't know anything about a horse's mind.

When I was about six, the rodeo came to Vancouver and my dad took me on the ferry over to the mainland to see it. I met my first cowboy at that rodeo — a Native, dark as mahogany. He was wearing a purple satin shirt, and when he lifted me up and stuck me on the saddle, I said to myself, *This is it.* That saddle was where I was meant to be.

My dad usually kept two or three ponies of his own — mostly cayuses (low-quality horses) — for playing polo on. Dad was always scuffling around looking for pasture for his polo horses, and I remember them being tethered around the open fields surrounding our house.

I was scared to death the first time a horse broke into a

Me at nine. (COURTESY IAN TYSON)

lope while I was being ponied by my dad. When you're a little kid, it feels like you're way up in the sky on that saddle. Some people give up altogether after a scare like that, just as some people give up on hockey the first time they're checked into the boards. Not me. I got back on.

The old man was always on the lookout for a cheap horse, and I encountered more Native cowboys on trips up into the British Columbia interior with him. We'd head off to Clinton or 100 Mile House and stay at dude ranches and reservations. The cowboy culture in British Columbia those days was heavily Native, and the colourful characters fascinated me. Their demeanour was so different from the suits in Victoria, and they also worked with their hands like the labourers I admired. The Natives would cowboy in the summer and in the winter they'd work as loggers. That Native cowboy culture I knew as a kid is now gone, completely gone.

Some people are born to live with horses and others aren't. I believe that with my whole heart and soul. I know ranch families in which one kid can't wait to be a cowboy and the other kid is counting the minutes until he can get the hell off that ranch and never come back. They're both growing up in the same environment, but one kid is born to be with horses and the other isn't. In my family, Jean had a passing interest in horses, but I was the one born to live with them. It's in my genetic makeup. Simple as that.

As kids, Jean and I spent our summers at my maternal grandmother's three-storey summer home on a small farm at Cadboro Bay — the same place my mom was staying when she first met my dad — a few miles up the coast from our place. (My mom's siblings had all left Victoria by then, which meant we were the only ones around to borrow the house.)

It was a wonderful place for a kid. My room, on the second floor, opened to the sea through a large half-moon aperture covered only by fly screening. The floor was corrugated tin that had warped considerably down through the years. Walking on it created a cacophony of metal sounds and rumblings, probably very much like an old ship. When I climbed into bed, I would fall asleep listening to the soft waves lapping on the shore of Cadboro Bay. The sound of the waves and the rumbling tin floor are still as vivid as yesterday.

The farm had apples, corn, peas, beans, a greenhouse with grapevines and a Jersey cow named Nelly. And, of course, my father's uninvited guests: his horses. The in-laws didn't like the old man, and he didn't like them much either. They were Scots Presbyterians and he was a Brit, and they regarded him as a man of no account. I think he just dumped his horses, Ginger and Steel, in with the Jersey cow until he rented a nearby pasture with a barn, a stable and a big chestnut tree right in the middle of the field. He always planned to buy that land but never got it done.

At Cadboro Bay I'd ride the old man's horses bareback, messing around trying to get them to do something athletic. They were gentle creatures but if you tormented them enough, they'd move. (Eventually I'd learn to ride bareback like a Comanche.) My dad loved to run his horses on the beach at Cadboro Bay, and I'd ride with him, happily galloping through the salty surf.

A laconic Chinese man named Lee cared for everything on the farm. We were very fond of each other, old Lee and I. He lived alone in a shack at the end of the lane that led to the backside of the farm. There he'd eat his meals of rice on the porch. Lee later claimed I knew how to speak Cantonese when I was very young, but I can't recall that.

I do remember, years later, his producing a nickel-plated Smith & Wesson .38 revolver from a hidden drawer in his table and giving the gun to my father. Many Chinese lived on the island, and the tongs — secret societies for Chinese immigrants — were ever present. Most of their members were gamblers, and I guess Lee was too, but I don't think he was in a tong. One of Lee's Chinese buddies had been murdered in a big wealthy house up the hill;

afterwards he obviously felt it was necessary to keep a gun. But its usefulness eventually passed, and that's when he handed it off to my dad. (He liked the old man a lot, just as he liked me.)

My only memory of the Second World War is at Cadboro Bay. There was an army base a couple of miles away at Gordon Head, and I remember the enlistees marching along the narrow country roads on hot summer days in 1940, when I was six years old. Jean and I took a break from fighting over Monopoly to stand at the side of the road with baskets of apples from our orchard, passing them to the tall soldiers as they marched past.

I got hooked on the cowboy way of life thanks to my dad's horses and the Will James books he gave me as presents. In the early 1940s the prolific James became *the* mythic western figure in North America, presenting himself as an authentic drifting cowboy from Montana. I was totally captivated by his highly skilled drawings and colourful stories of buckarooing in the West. His illustrations of horses in all kinds of action set him apart from other artists. James drew the western horse, the shaggy and unpredictable bronc, the precursor of what we know now as the American quarter horse — a small, strong horse bred for short bursts of speed. Nobody could draw them like Will James.

James's books came out at the rate of about two a year, giving the old man the perfect, inexpensive solution for his kid's birthday and Christmas needs. The wild tales totally captivated a whole generation of young gunsels — wannabe cowboys — including me. But even as a boy I sensed there was something wrong with James's stories. He never named any towns. He never named any actual ranches. His locations and geography were always vague. His fellow punchers seemed to have no surnames.

Years later, in 1967, when Nevada writer Anthony Amaral put out his book *Will James: The Gilt Edged Cowboy*, we Jamesian cowboys found out that our hero was actually Ernest Dufault from Quebec, who around 1907 had hopped on a train for Saskatchewan and set about learning the cowboy trade. He soon drifted south across the porous Saskatchewan–Montana border, renamed himself Will James and worked hard at leaving his accent behind and reinventing himself as the quintessential drifting cowboy.

As his fame grew, so did his fear of being exposed. He must have bought into the Texas myth that real cowboys were all third or fourth generation, born and bred in the West, even though there were lots of legitimate cowboys from other places — including France. At one point James even tried to have the official records of his birth destroyed. He used to explain the remnants of his Québécois accent by saying that after his parents were killed, a French-Canadian trapper had adopted him. James wasn't an honest guy. None of us are, but he didn't want to admit to any of the facts about his life.

He also claimed to be a great bronc rider, and to this day nobody really knows if he was any good or not. He had a lie for everything, but the son of a gun could draw. I wrote a song about him in the 1980s ("Will James"):

I've memorized those pictures, boys,
They're still the very best,

If whiskey was his mistress,
His true love was the West.

There's a lot of love and sympathy for James in that song, and there's definitely a lot of me in those last couple of lines too.

After James became successful, he went to Hollywood and hung out with Tom Mix, Yakima Canutt and all the other cowboys. They made tons of money and partied all the time. James's drinking got heavier and heavier, and his life started to unravel. When I met western actor and stuntman Dick Farnsworth at a Wild West event in Princeton, B.C., years later, I asked him whether he'd ever met Will James.

"I did," he said.

"Did he have a Québécois accent?"

"No, he sounded like a Texas cowboy to me. But you know, when I met him, he was so drunk he pissed himself. He was wearing a black suit and he pissed himself."

James drank himself to death in 1942, the year I turned nine.

Around this time I first encountered western music on our old wooden tube radio. I distinctly remember taking a wire connected to the back of the radio and grounding it on the iron radiator. Somehow I picked up WSM's broadcast of the Grand Ole Opry from Nashville, and I listened intently as Roy Acuff sang "Wreck on the Highway." The wailing, keening sound of the dobro guitar really blew me away. I'd never heard anything like that before — that high, lonesome sound.

I'd had no real access to western music before that. Most of my friends were into the pop music of the time. In our home, music consisted of my dad singing in the shower and my mother playing classical music on the piano. She'd once had ambitions to become a concert pianist and had studied piano in New York for a season, but she just didn't have the chops. Later in life she developed a hand condition that forced her to stop playing, and she gave up her music dreams. As for me, back then I had no aspirations whatsoever of becoming a professional singer. I sang along with the music on the radio, but that was it.

A couple of years after I first heard Roy Acuff, I went to a Saturday afternoon matinee with a friend to see Tex Ritter and his horse White Flash, along with the original Sons of the Pioneers, at the Rio, an old vaudeville theatre on Government Street downtown that had been converted into a movie house. This was in the mid-1940s, when the Saturday afternoon western movie matinee was at its peak, and we kids loved seeing Gene Autry and Roy Rogers on the Rio's big screen. My friends and I went to the movies by ourselves and no one thought anything of it. We would roam all over Victoria — into the woods, through the fields, downtown — without anybody worrying about us. It was a different time.

I don't know how we found out about the Tex Ritter show, but I've carried the memory of the experience with me into adulthood. The 450-seat theatre was half full — all boys, Saturday afternoon western movie freaks like myself. The show's primary draw was Tex Ritter and White Flash, but the Sons of the Pioneers stole the show. Their harmonies resonated strongly in my twelve-year-old ears, though I didn't know what they were doing. It was the original group, with Bob Nolan, Tim Spencer and the Farr brothers. I don't think anybody can do harmonies better than those guys did.

Bob Nolan was a pretty imposing figure standing there at the microphone with his arm crooked, displaying the many mother-of-pearl buttons running up the sleeve of his tailored western shirt (I think the shirts impressed me as much as the music). Afterwards Tex Ritter rode out onstage on old White Flash and sang in his great baritone voice.

I don't know why the Sons of the Pioneers and Tex Ritter came to Victoria — probably for an el cheapo publicity tour. It would have been a unique musical act for the city; the bands of the day were imitation society bands that played dance music with as much sophistication as they could muster, which wasn't very much.

After the show my dad asked me, "You want to go see that horse?"

I didn't need to think. "Sure."

Turns out White Flash was stabled at the Willows Racetrack, near our place. A cowboy let me sit on the horse, and I felt a big rush as I settled into Tex Ritter's silver-mounted saddle. For a horse-crazy kid like me, that was as good as it could get.

At the end of the Second World War and the beginning of my teenage years, we moved to a funny little Oak Bay house on Wilmot Place, a beautiful street lined with oak and walnut trees. The window of my bedroom was ideal for sneaking out — I could get onto the sloping roof and then drop down to the ground. We lived next door to a Gothic mansion with a big wooded area that abutted our back door, and I would drop into those trees to meet my friend Bugs Bigelow at night. He was a big, tough kid, wilder than hell, and we'd go knock off a few candy bars from the local confectionary.

Bugsy and I were constantly getting into trouble together. Sometimes my parents would catch me sneaking out to meet him. They put up a pretty concerned front, but I don't recall them laying down the law. They were just trying to hold on to me so I could make it through adolescence without getting myself killed.

My parents sent me to all-boys private schools, which meant that when I hit puberty and became interested in girls, I'd had little contact with them. I first masturbated to Émile Zola's *Nana*. How I came into possession of that book I haven't a clue. But in my upstairs bedroom under the eaves of that little house on Wilmot Place, I had my first orgasm, inspired by the passage where a beautiful Nana stands naked before a warming fire, displaying her voluptuousness. I was thirteen, full of adolescent angst, excitement and wonder. Getting off was a big deal, second only to the real thing (still a couple of years down the road).

Though widely practised, jacking off was not widely discussed by us boys. It was performed under the covers and was nobody else's business. Still, I was proud to be pleasuring myself to classic literature rather than cheap pornography or the trashy paperbacks of the 1940s, stuff like Irving Shulman's *The Amboy Dukes*. I viewed my choice of *Nana* as an indication of my superior taste in literature.

The years at Wilmot Place were a challenging time for our family. I think Dad felt that he was stuck in the insurance business and that he wasn't very good at it. After the war everybody was lining up to buy their postwar cars. Some of the old man's buddies were becoming very successful car dealers, and he felt that he was missing out. While they were making a pile of money, my dad was eagerly awaiting his inheritance, like a typical Englishman. But thanks to the longevity of my grandfather, my dad didn't cash in until much later in life. And by then the inheritance had been whittled down to a modest sum that he used to pay off some bills and buy a new car.

Dad was always bitching about having to go up the coast for work. I think he had a girlfriend on the east side of the island, at Ladysmith, but that's conjecture. Jean thinks he did too. We didn't suspect that anything was going on back then; it's something we surmised later on while reminiscing about his trips. We even think we know who the girlfriend was; when I was in my twenties, Dad asked me to look her up for some kind of horse deal. I ended up meeting her a few times — a tall lady with dark hair and thick glasses.

While Dad complained about the insurance business, I was having a rough time at home too. As a young boy I had always got along with the old man, but in my teenage years we started to fight, mostly about trivial things like my messy hair or muddy boots. It got really bad, sometimes to the verge of violence. My mother tried to be the U.N. envoy but it didn't work.

Jean and I were both suffering from island claustrophobia — we wanted to get the hell away from home. The only problem was that neither of us knew where the hell we wanted to go. There was nothing rational about our rebellion; it was just hormonal. When Jean was thirteen, my parents sent her to Shawnigan Lake School, a private boarding school located between Duncan and Victoria. She didn't enjoy that at all. She too had a difficult adolescence.

In 1949, when I was fifteen, I got to escape the island for a summer by working in the mountain town of Banff, Alberta. My aunt Mame worked at the Banff Springs Hotel as a hostess during the tourist season. Through her I got a job working on a pack string for outdoor adventure freaks, back and forth to Mount Assiniboine, on the Alberta–B.C. border.

There were only two ways to reach Mount Assiniboine back then: by foot or on horseback. Helicopters weren't an option. We'd start at Brewster Creek, a few miles outside of Banff, and head south up the creek. The weather was treacherous out there. Often we'd start off with a lovely morning, then by eleven o'clock it would be snowing and we'd be freezing cold. It was fine if you were dressed properly, but I never was. Whenever we encountered cowboys coming from the B.C. side of the mountain with their pack strings, I was jealous of their good saddles, slickers and hats. I was just grubbing along.

I worked under Erling Strom, a fabled mountaineer and ski guide. He didn't like cowboys much but he needed them, since he had a whole string of horses. He'd usually hire an experienced cowboy and two gunsels. The experienced cowboy's name was Al Johnson and he became one of my early mentors, teaching me all about packing and shoeing horses.

After a day of travel we'd overnight at the halfway cabin, a gorgeous jewel of a place tucked away in an alpine meadow.

The packer — that was me — was responsible for preparing supper. Looking back, the thought of me at fifteen cooking for all those tourists is ridiculous. The bread was all crushed from being packed on horses, and I relied entirely on a can opener for those meals.

At night I'd sleep in the saddle shack under the sweaty horse blankets. It was a pretty unsophisticated setup, but I didn't care. I was in the Rockies with horses — what more could I ask for? The next day we'd leave the halfway cabin, go over a couple of mountain passes, cross a big alpine basin and finally reach Mount Assiniboine.

My dad didn't at all understand what I was doing in Banff. The leisure industry was just taking off, and he thought my work was going to be like Alberta in 1906, when he froze his ass off. He didn't understand how I could run packhorses and come back with money in my pocket. In his mind the only way to make money was through drudgery — selling insurance or cars. You could ride horses for your own amusement, but that was it.

The notion that somebody could make a living playing music was even more foreign to him. Everything I would end up doing in life was part of the leisure industry that my dad couldn't wrap his head around. Today, of course, that industry is responsible for countless jobs, but during my old man's childhood there wasn't any of that. There were no outdoor adventurers paying guides to take them deep into the mountains, nor were there cowboys hauling their horses around in trailers behind their trucks. When I drive from my place into Calgary, I'll see about twenty of those trailers — and that's all part of the leisure industry.

My dad had always admired the cowboy life, but he was

scared that if I became a cowboy I'd be as unsuccessful as he'd been at it. He worried that I was frittering my life away. "You'll end up with a worn-out saddle and an empty whiskey bottle," he'd say. It was kind of true, but I didn't hear him when he said it — I'd tuned him out.

When I returned home after my summer in Banff, my dad and I continued to fight. Eventually it got so bad that my parents made me board at the all-boys school I had been attending. Then I really went nuts. It was just a place where people who had enough money could send their incorrigible kids. Schools like that are completely different now, co-ed and scholastically sound, but back then it seemed to me that the administrators didn't give a shit about whether you learned anything or not; they just took your parents' money. The good students learned and the bad ones didn't, and all of us had to eat the lousy food.

We chased girls when we could but there wasn't much opportunity for that, since the school wasn't co-ed. We had one co-ed dance, a weird event for us boys. I danced with this one girl I was smitten with, but I knew nothing about dancing. There was no music program at the school; instead we had programs such as rugby, boxing and rifle practice — an educational opportunity that's made life hard for the gophers on my ranch. But with no arts program, I had no idea how to dance. We just walked on each other's feet.

In class I stared out the window and daydreamed. I was good at sports because I was athletically more gifted than most of the kids, but when the other kids started working harder, I didn't, and I started getting beat. I wasn't bearing down on anything.

My friend Bugsy got sent to the same boarding school, which meant we kept getting into trouble together. We were both good at sports, but he hurt his back, which finished him. I blew my knee out, which ended football for me too. If you were helping the school on the sports field, then they cut you some slack, but after we got injured, the free ride was over.

The headmaster didn't believe in sparing the rod. He beat up on us kids with a switch. If we caused any trouble, down came our pants. I got sixteen lashes one time along with Bugsy, probably for stealing change in the locker rooms or sneaking out at night. I think we held the record for most cuts from the cane. They really laid it on, leaving big welts on our asses. I think they even drew blood from Bugsy. They thought they could break us through force, but it didn't work.

We kept getting in trouble at home in Victoria too. When I was about sixteen, Bugsy and I borrowed my mom's car after we got drunk. I missed a curb and crashed the car into a stone wall, severely denting Mom's vehicle. She was very upset and I felt pretty bad about the whole thing.

I don't remember my graduation ceremony. What I do know is that the staff of the boarding school had definitely had their fill of Ian Tyson and Bugsy Bigelow. We were *persona non grata* and they wanted us out of there. So we left.

CHAPTER 3

Drifting

Through my late teens I drifted aimlessly. After spending a couple of weeks at Victoria College (I decided the academic life wasn't for me), I got a job at an Esquimalt sawmill. I worked the midnight shift, sorting two-by-fours and other raw lumber off the green chain. It was a tough job and I worked hard at it until the sawmill laid me off, just a few weeks after I started. After that I knew I didn't want to do hard labour all the time, but I still didn't have a clue what I wanted to do. I wasn't lazy, just restless. I lacked focus. The concept of applying myself to reaching a specific goal was completely foreign to me.

In 1952, when I was eighteen, my parents, Jean and I took a trip to England to visit relatives. Old George wanted to reconnect with Grandpa and check up on his inheritance. The trip was a pretty dour affair. The war still felt pretty fresh and the food was awful. I love the English, but that wasn't the England of today.

For me the highlight of the trip was discovering the

basement clubs on Oxford Street in London, the brassy girls and the guys with their drainpipe pants and long sideburns. I can still remember the stale beer smell that pervaded those places. The whole Teddy Boy scene was just taking off and the bands weren't yet into the blues rock they did so well later on. When we were there the big thing was skiffle, a hokey combination of country and Dixieland. But still I thought I'd like to play drums in one of those bands. On the boat ride back to Canada I befriended the orchestra drummer. He worked very hard at selling me a set of drums but never got it done.

After the trip Jean returned to England, where she married a guy who'd followed her from Victoria. (They had four daughters before they split up.) We didn't see each other much for a long while after she left home, but we became very good friends later in life. She lives in Victoria, where Dad and Mom stayed put until they died in 1966 and 1984 respectively. Jean and I visited Smugglers Cove after Mom died, letting the wind take her ashes out into the Strait of Juan de Fuca.

After I got back from England in 1952, I drifted into the B.C. bush, landing a job with the provincial forest service, first at Port Alberni, on Vancouver Island, and later at Harrison Lake, on the mainland. The forestry work didn't interest me very much. I took humidity readings and did odd jobs such as mowing lawns, and I'd do the occasional stretch on a lookout when a regular got injured or went nuts, as some of them did.

I kept causing trouble at Port Alberni by stealing away to dances at nearby Beaver Creek. I wasn't allowed to use the government trucks but I drove them a couple of times anyway, disconnecting the odometer so nobody could tell I'd put on any miles. I thought it was a good plan, but one time the odometer cord was swinging under the dash and hit metal, blowing out all the fuses. Despite my shenanigans I never got fired. I was a pretty likeable kid, so my bosses would just roll their eyes.

All the island dances I went to in my early years have been puréed into one vague memory that involves a piano, an accordion and a fiddle — all of them out of tune. The dances were pretty wanting musically, but we had a good time anyway. At Beaver Creek I met Annie Kalugin, a compact, good-looking Ukrainian gal. I had the hots for her and did my best to get into her pants. She liked me a lot too, but not enough to give up her virginity.

We had a lot of downtime at the forest service since we were basically on call 24/7. I spent most of that time reading and daydreaming about girls and rodeos and bucking horses. That's when I got bit by the rodeo bug. I wanted to be a saddle bronc rider but couldn't afford the saddle, so instead I made myself a pair of bronc chaps in do-it-yourself gunsel style. I had no idea what I was doing, but I got a pattern from somebody and cut out the chaps from reddish purple leather, holding the pieces together with rivets and stitching. Then I added some white lettering with my initials.

Next I got a set of Jerry Ambler–style Crockett spurs and borrowed a Dixon bareback rigging. At nineteen I rode in my first rodeo in Duncan, on Vancouver Island. It was a small-time rodeo, but for us rubes on the island it was a big deal. All the Natives came and Dave Perry from Cache Creek won all the money. As for me, I didn't fall off the horse — I was hooked after that. My old man even showed up. Being a cowboy at heart, he got a great kick out of watching me ride.

After that first rodeo, my logger friends and I would go to other rodeos in the B.C. interior when we had the spare time, scraping together the fifteen bucks we needed to enter. I'd always run into Annie's three brothers, the Kalugins, at the various rodeos. They were small, friendly guys who wore funny old-fashioned hats — little munchkin-type characters, almost like cartoons. I wish I'd spent more time with the Kalugins, but I got transferred to Harrison Lake pretty soon after I got to know them. Somebody gave me a horse at Harrison Lake but I didn't have a well-fenced area to keep him in; after he trashed a couple of vegetable gardens I had to get rid of him.

I kept rodeoing after my transfer. In those days locals could enter the pro rodeos. The hometown boys acted as cannon fodder — or comic relief — before the pros came out. I local-entried all over the place, so Ian Tyson ended up being a "local boy" from a lot of different towns.

I described the key to riding in a 1964 piece for *Maclean's* magazine: "Good rodeo riding is, like most other sports, a matter of timing. The rider has to find his horse's rhythm and swing with it for the whole ride. In saddle-bronc riding, the cowboy makes a series of sweeps, or 'licks,' with both spurs, from the horse's shoulders back to the cantle board, a piece of wood that sticks up in the air from the rear of the saddle. The licks are timed to the horse's jumps — one jump, one lick — and there are about ten licks in the ten seconds he's supposed to stay on board. . . . Most of the horses are psychotic farm animals although a few are genuinely wild ones. Both kinds usually survive in rodeo longer

Bronc-riding at the rodeo in Cloverdale, B.C., in 1955. (COURTESY IAN TYSON)

than the riders." Nowadays I wouldn't call farm animals psychotic — I'd call 'em spoiled.

I was basically an amateur who had a lot of fun. I couldn't ride a really rank one, although I know cowboys who still think I was once a great bronc rider. They've made it all up in their minds. They wanted me to be a great rider, so I was. I know one cowboy who swears I rode with him at this rodeo years ago, had this great ride and so on. In reality I wasn't even there.

While working for the forest service, I decided to apply to the Vancouver School of Art (now the Emily Carr University of Art + Design). As a kid I could always draw, right from the beginning. Inspired by Will James, I'd draw horses,

horses and more horses. There was one exception: when I was eleven or twelve I entered an airplane-drawing contest and won. Drawing has always been present in my life, but as a kid I had no aspirations of becoming a great artist.

Now, in my late teens, I wondered if horseback life and the art world could be compatible, and even energize one another creatively. The possibilities in my head were very vague at the time but, unbeknownst to me, Joe Beeler was thinking along the same lines in Arizona. He'd go on to co-found Cowboy Artists of America, a group that would become hugely successful, as would Joe. We didn't know it back then, but by mixing horses and art we were precursors of the cowboy renaissance that would sweep the West thirty years later.

Marrying cowboys with art wasn't exactly new; Charles M. Russell, the greatest western painter of them all, was doing it way back in the 1880s. But while today it's easy to find probably twenty different Charlie Russell art books — full of scenes with violent action upfront and, in the distance, faraway mountains diffused with blue and rose — Charlie's work was still pretty underground when I applied to art school in the 1950s.

I'd discovered Charlie in Victoria, after my summer wrangling in Banff in the late 1940s. I had come back with something like fifteen cavities and had to go get them fixed. In those days it was a painful business. The dentist's office had an old, beat-up copy of *Good Medicine*, a book of Charlie's illustrated letters, full of cowboys and Indians and coyotes and horses. *This guy's even better than Will James*, I thought. I loved that book. *Good Medicine* got me through all that drilling.

Somehow, at twenty-one, I got accepted into art school, so in the fall of 1954 I moved to Vancouver. The whole city was basically made of wood back then — a damp, mouldy place. I rented a room in an old boarding house in the west end, the area where most of the other students lived. Our rooms had hotplates in them but usually no fridge. It was pretty primitive, nothing like the glitzy high-rises of today.

The Vancouver School of Art was very post-impressionist in the 1950s, as I quickly found out. Literal art such as Charlie Russell's — the stuff I liked — was very much frowned upon. Instead we studied the cubists, the abstract expressionists and the post-impressionists.

I shared studio space in a big old dilapidated wooden building near Victory Square with Nancy Patterson, a brilliant artist who won all the scholarships. I couldn't come close to competing with Nancy as a painter, since she was miles ahead and actually applied herself to her craft. Instead I hung out with her boyfriend, Gordie Cox, a stocky little disbarred jockey and wannabe hipster from Hamilton, Ontario. While Nancy diligently worked on her art, Gordie and I occupied our time by goofing off and stealing jars of peanut butter from the stores on Robson Street. We were poor art students, living from hand to mouth.

Whenever we got some money, we'd go to beer parlours where the waiters had to buy beer from the bartender and sell it around the room, carrying it on wide-rimmed trays. All the beer parlours had a side for men and a side for "ladies and escorts," based on a weird puritanical take on morality. And there was absolutely no music, not even a jukebox. The beer parlours were very controlled — you didn't bend the rules in there. If a Native man got out of line, all the waiters would put down their trays and converge on the poor bastard, kicking the living shit out of him before throwing him in the alley and returning to work. They didn't fart around or even bother calling the cops. They took care of it themselves.

I mostly went through art school the same way I went through high school — daydreaming. Most of my effort focused on a spectacularly beautiful Greek girl who came to the school a year after I enrolled. Dark, gorgeous and wild, Evinia arrived in Vancouver fresh from Vernon, where she'd broken hearts the length and breadth of the Okanagan Valley. With her jet black hair and dark eyes, she looked like a Bollywood star. Her dad, Curly, was an iconic guy in the Okanagan, a classic immigrant success story. He had arrived in Canada with no money and started a Greek cafe in Vernon, which eventually became profitable. He and his wife had just the one daughter, and they gave her everything she could possibly want. She came to Vancouver driving a brand new Impala convertible that her daddy had bought her.

She was like me, like the rest of us — trying to figure out who she was and where the hell she wanted to go. It didn't take long for Evinia and me to fall for each other. We had a volatile love affair that ultimately ended in a catastrophic breakup. I'd also been trying to get into the pants of another spectacular-looking art student — and I succeeded. When Evinia found out about my shenanigans, she broke it off and split for California without finishing art school. She was very hurt. Evinia was an accomplished heartbreaker, but she didn't like being on the other end.

Evinia remains an amazingly beautiful woman and, some fifty-five years later, we're still friends and soulmates.

I've had my women and she's had her men, but since that first breakup we've never gotten jealous about each other's romantic involvements over the years. We've remained buddies through it all.

All through art school I worked odd jobs off and on, anything I could do to get by. I bused tables at the Terminal City Club, an upscale businessmen's establishment (much later I would return there as a star performer). During the summer breaks I returned to Banff, this time to drive cabs and small buses for Brewster, the tourism outfit I'd worked on the pack string for when I was fifteen. In my downtime I'd go to the Rundle Rock paint shop, across from the entrance to the Banff Springs Hotel. That's where all the other employees — mostly students, like me — hung out waiting for calls, and while we waited, we played blackjack. Those games went on 24/7. Most of my pay was gambled and gone come September, thanks to cards (that's where my song "Summer Wages" came from).

Brewster's dispatcher, Rod Adams, was a gruff, tough character right out of the movies. "Tyson," he'd bark from behind his desk, "get down to the train station for a pickup!" In addition to his dispatching duties, Rod also made sure the blackjack games didn't get totally out of control. And if anyone wanted time off, they had to go through him.

Rod liked cowboys, and one day in 1956 I asked him, "Can I get off for a day and go to a rodeo?" That request would completely change my life, though I didn't know it at the time.

He grunted his response. "I guess you can go."

"Can I have the fifteen bucks I need to enter?"

Sure enough, Rod kindly covered my entry fee, and a girl who worked at the Banff Springs Hotel drove me to the Dogpound Rodeo near Cremona, a little farm town north of Calgary. When we arrived under a grey sky, I entered as a local, as usual.

Soon the rain started pouring down, soaking my big thoroughbred mare. We came out of the chute and I started fine, but the rigging shifted too far forward on her withers. I spurred off to the side and landed on my feet. What happened next was a complete fluke.

The rankest saddle bronc will not step on a person. Unlike bulls, horses abhor stepping on a human body. They might kick you in the air as you're coming down, but they won't step on you. But this time my ankle, her foot and the ground collided — and my ankle exploded. I knew right away that it was gone.

"Would one of you guys give me a hand?"

I got no sympathy from the other cowboys. "You're not hurt," they said.

The girl from the Banff Springs drove me into Calgary to the old General Hospital, where the doctors cut off my boot before operating on my ankle, sticking in a few pins. These were the early days of metal reconstruction but those doctors did a fine job. That mare had really messed up my ankle and the operation couldn't have been easy. I have the pins in my ankle to this day.

After the surgery I was put in the broken leg ward for two weeks, along with a telephone lineman and a couple of other cowboys. The kid in the bed next to me had a guitar, and I started to learn this song I kept hearing on the radio. The singer was an Arkansas-born guy, about my age, whose name was Johnny Cash. The song that kept playing on the radio started like this: *I keep a close watch on this heart of mine . . .*

It was 1956, I was twenty-two years old and "I Walk the Line" was huge — but hard to learn on the guitar. It had a few key changes, which was unusual for country music of that time. The song also had a very distinct picking style. Later, when I went to New York, nobody played that way. Joan Baez and the other folksingers did Carter scratch, where you're playing with your fingers. But Johnny Cash's guys, the Tennessee Two, played a very simple percussive style with a flat pick. That's exactly how I started playing, learning by trial and error in that broken leg ward until I could keep up with Johnny.

Before I found myself in that Calgary hospital, I never had any idea of seriously learning music. I had tried a little guitar when I was younger but, as usual, I didn't take the trouble to apply myself. I often wonder what direction I'd have gone in had I started playing in my teenage years. I got a real late start, but in those days guitar players weren't a dime a dozen as they are now, so being a late bloomer didn't set me too far back.

Music absorbed me in a very gradual way. I belonged to a generation that was waking up to music in the 1950s, and I'd gotten interested in jazz and big bands while working in the forest service. I remember piling into somebody's car and going to hear Tommy Dorsey's big band in Vancouver, driving all the way down from Harrison Lake. There were no bridges across the Fraser River then, so we had to take a ferry, all the loggers standing on deck in their black mohair suits. Tommy Dorsey absolutely blew us away. That was probably a sixteen-piece orchestra, and Tommy Dorsey was a great trombone and trumpet player. I think Gene Krupa was on drums. On another trip we heard Stan Kenton with his big band.

And then there was Rolly Borhaven, a handsome logger I'd met. He wore a moustache and goatee and had that whole Prince Valiant look of the time. Rolly was a lady-killer and played the guitar. We'd spend a lot of our free time at the legion halls, and invariably Rolly would get up with his guitar and sing Wilf Carter. Carter was the folk superstar of the time, with his original guitar style and wonderful voice, clean and pure as the Rocky Mountains. His songs were ridiculously corny — *There's a love knot in my lariat*, for example — but melodically brilliant. His sound was like no other, and it seemed to come right out of the high country.

By the time I had enrolled at art school, rockabilly was the big thing, a tectonic musical shift from jazz. I remember hearing Bill Haley and His Comets play "Rock Around the Clock" in the 1955 movie *Blackboard Jungle*. That had a huge impact on me — I can hear that snare sound to this day. That simple southern rockabilly was like nothing else I'd heard. It was open-chord guitar, a big change from the jazz guitarists, who all played closed chords, bar chords, suspended chords and diminished chords. Bill Haley and the rockabilly guys were playing open G and C chords, the ringing stuff. I was totally into rockabilly before I thought anything about folk. Hell, I didn't even know what folk was.

After Elvis broke out in 1956, I realized I could sing. I loved Elvis's style. No white kid had ever sung like that before, and I found that I could imitate him pretty accurately.

In art school, before I broke my ankle, I'd played a few gigs with Taller O'Shea, a small-time West Coast bandleader. His band would travel the Native reserve circuit; they played a kind of mutated western swing with a lot of Ukrainian content and Wilf Carter influence. It was a distinctly Canadian sound and I didn't dig it that much, but Steve Cresta, a sometime art student, played accordion in O'Shea's band and got me the gig. I knew about three chords. The only reason they let me join the band was because I could sing and was a good-looking kid. I played a few gigs with a few other bands as well — band members were always changing around, and everybody knew each other — but never anything too serious.

By the time I got discharged from the broken leg ward in Calgary with pins embedded in my ankle, I could play more than three chords. I convalesced at my parents' place out at Mount Tolmie on Vancouver Island for a few weeks before returning to Vancouver for the fall semester. Once back at art school, I really wanted to be part of the music scene. I bought a cheap Hofner guitar from a pawnshop on East Hastings and kept practising.

Pretty soon I was playing in a rockabilly band. Radio stations were all jumping on the rockabilly bandwagon, and the DJs would put together bands, sending them out to play high schools on weekends. The big DJ in Vancouver was Red Robinson of CKWX. With my playing improved, I joined one of Red's four-piece bands, the Sensational Stripes.

We did a handful of gigs, including two or three high school dances. We also opened for Buddy Holly once, because it was a union requirement that a local band had to open for the big acts. Eddie Cochran also played that show.

I loved the rockabilly scene but my tenure with the Sensational Stripes was short-lived. The girls seemed to like me more than Jimmy Morrison, the kid who fronted the band by imitating Elvis. My good looks got in the way of his success, so he went and fired me for it — at least, that's how I'm telling it.

In my last year of art school, in 1958, the coffeehouse scene started blooming in Vancouver and everywhere else. The folk seeds were being sown. Roy Guest, an English guy I met, got me my first coffeehouse gig at this little place he'd opened called the Heidelberg. Roy was one of those guys who bummed around the world with his guitar. I don't know how the hell I got through the first gigs. I didn't know anything, but Roy taught me a couple of folk songs and encouraged me to keep at it.

Finally I started getting gigs in Chinatown, at the Smilin' Buddha Cabaret on East Hastings. There were a few cabarets like that in the area, and they weren't like the beer parlours at all; the cabarets had live music, dancing and hookers. I remember one of the hookers introducing me to B.B. King's music for the first time. I loved it, of course — my ears were open.

After a while, a rockabilly Chuck Berry–styled guitar player I'd met—I think his name was Johnny Rommis— gave me a bit of career advice. I had the ducktail haircut and all that shit, and he thought I was a good-looking kid who could really make it in music.

"You can't do it here, though," he told me. "You'll have to go somewhere else."

"Where?"

"L.A. or Chicago. Toronto maybe."

So that's what I did. At Easter in 1958 I got drunk with my friend Ron Cameron and another buddy, and Ron conjured up an idea. "Let's bugger off to California in my Dodge."

We agreed that we would visit Evinia in L.A. — we were corresponding off and on — and took along our copies of Jack Kerouac's *On the Road*. That book came out right when I was in the middle of art school, and it hit me and my associates big time. Kerouac's road had western tinges to it, and I used to go to rodeos with that book packed in my rigging bag. I was a beatnik cowboy, I guess. I liked the idea of being an outsider hipster who loved literature and music but lived the outlaw life.

I don't know where we got the gas money, but we drove Ron's Dodge all the way to the Grapevine — the long grade between Bakersfield, California, and L.A. That's where the car died. We decided to split up to hitchhike the rest of the way.

I stuck out my thumb and a rather cool-looking dude in a sedan stopped to pick me up. He wore a classy tan corduroy suit and cowboy boots.

"You a cowboy?" he asked. I was wearing a straw hat.

"Well, I'd like to be."

"What happened?"

I said our car died.

"Can you ride?"

"Sure, I can ride."

"My name's Sam, and we're doing a television series next week out at RKO Studios. Brand-new series called *The Rifleman*. I think it's going to be a winner. I could probably help you out, get you a job riding up and down the street as an extra."

I never went, but I later learned that the Sam I met that day was former *Gunsmoke* scriptwriter Sam Peckinpah, who went on do classic westerns such as *Ride the High Country* and *The Wild Bunch*. Years later, in the early 1970s, at a get-together in Durango, Mexico, during the filming of *Pat Garrett and Billy the Kid* with Bob Dylan and Kris Kristofferson, I met Sam again. He remembered the whole hitchhiking episode. I was going to ride in that movie, but I got deathly sick on the plane going down. Again I had missed a chance to be in one of Peckinpah's productions.

I eventually made it to L.A. and met up with Evinia. By this time I had started to realize I had been an asshole and I wanted to repair the damage. But too much damage had been done. We had a big fight, so I thumbed my way back to Vancouver and art school. I made it back in record time — about two days.

By this time I was really sliding off the dime and not taking care of my art. In order to graduate and get a diploma, each student had to put on an art show. I could barely do it. I didn't have enough material because I was always off playing guitar. But somehow I cobbled something together, enough to graduate in 1958.

I did learn a bit about line and composition in art school. Even though I was goofing off all the time, I absorbed a lot by osmosis. It took decades before I figured out that I had actually learned about aesthetics during those years. I also became an admirer of the French impressionists as well as Charlie Russell.

After graduation I went pipelining west of Kamloops with my friend Jack Bruce, a skiing star from Banff I'd met while working for Brewster. He drove one of the big buses and I got to know him over the card table in the paint shop. (Jack somehow eventually met Evinia through me and they were married for a short time. She had many husbands and men afterwards, but she had her only child with Jack.)

I kept rodeoing while Jack and I pipelined. At the end of the season I got laid off. The labour foreman, an American guy from Washington, owned a ranch nearby. "Can you start some broncs?" he asked me, referring to the initial training of unbroken horses.

"Sure I can," I answered, full of hubris and bravado.

I must have convinced him. Pretty soon I found myself batching it, breaking colts up at Deadman Creek. They must have been pretty gentle ponies — otherwise I could have got myself killed. I didn't know anything about breaking horses and it was just dumb luck that got me through. I got 'em rode, though I don't think I had much to teach them. It would have been wonderful if I'd had some experienced old hand to work with, but I had to teach myself. The experience gave me some lines for my song about Will James that I wrote in the 1980s:

A city kid, I asked myself
Now what would Will James do?

And you know it was the damnedest thing
But it kinda got me through

It's true. I just saddled them up and bumbled around as best I could. It was a start, and I've met lots of guys who had similar experiences. ("How'd you learn the trade?" I ask. "Just basic Will James," they say.)

I spent about two weeks at Deadman Creek, but soon I was headed down to L.A. again. Somewhere south of the border, near Blaine, Washington, a cool old French-Canadian bootlegger offered me a ride.

"Where you headed?" I asked.

"I'm going east, Dean." (The guy called me Dean because he couldn't say *Ian*.) So I went east with him, drifting as always. The French Canadian and I laid over in Miles City, Montana, while he got his car fixed — a stay I'll never forget, even though it was only a few days. In the 1950s Miles City was a hardcore cowtown; it had its own whiskey row, a long strip of old saloons. It was like walking into *Lonesome Dove*. The saloons were packed with bartenders and cowboys and whores, and they were all playing poker constantly. Everyone used big silver dollars to buy their whiskey. Fights would break out here and there. It was the quintessential West — the whole town was going full blast. It was the first time I'd seen a place like that. There was certainly no place like it anywhere in Canada.

Miles City made a huge impression on a kid who would eventually write and sing about the West. I wouldn't see Miles City again until I was a cowboy star, almost forty years later, and it was quite a disappointment. They're pretty redneck there, and the authentic cowtown flavour has been replaced by McDonalds and Subways. But back in the 1950s it was the old Montana.

During that layover waiting for the car, someone offered me a job breaking broncs up on the Missouri River. It's a good thing I didn't take it, because this time I probably would have got killed. Instead I kept drifting east with the French Canadian. We wound up in Chicago, where he had relatives. I was flat broke and he kindly drove me all the way to Windsor, where he bought me a bus ticket to Toronto.

After I got off the bus in Toronto, I called my mother and she sent me some money. Within days I landed a short-lived job at the *Star Weekly*, where I drew a few cowboy illustrations for novelettes the magazine was publishing. At night I played the coffeehouses.

In 1958 the coffeehouse scene was really taking off in Toronto, to the point where the city had more coffeehouses than folksingers. The demand far exceeded the supply, so I had no shortage of gigs. I was living high on the hog, considering that I got paid fifteen dollars a night and only had to pay seven bucks a week for rent.

After the illustrator gig I got a job as an artist in a glass factory, designing decorative art for peanut butter jars and Resdan shampoo bottles. I didn't have to be in until ten in the morning, which worked well for me, since I was singing at night. One day my shift foreman — a real nice Englishman — told me about this girl he'd heard down in Chatham, Ontario. "I was at this wild party on the weekend, and I met this lovely young lady singer. Absolutely terrific — and very unique. You should meet her."

"Sounds great." I was always keen on meeting girls, though I had a jealous Italian girlfriend, Michelle, at the time. But I wanted to meet this other girl, Sylvia Fricker, and hear this unique voice.

Sylvia ended up coming over to Michelle's folks' apartment, above a drycleaner on Avenue Road, where Michelle and I had shacked up for the weekend while her parents were away. Needless to say, Michelle was very upset about this pretty young folksinger intruding on her territory.

Sylvia impressed me from the start. She played this weird little mandocello — I'd never seen one before and don't think I've seen one since — and boy, could she sing. She could sing on pitch, which hardly anybody did in those days, because we didn't have monitors.

Pretty soon we were playing the Village Corner club on Avenue Road, a tiny brick house that became our main venue. That's where Ian & Sylvia broke out onto the Toronto scene. Red Shea played there once, and I remember him blowing us all out the damn door with his playing. Unlike the rest of us, he really knew how to play. (Years later he played guitar in my country-rock band Great Speckled Bird.)

In 1961 Ian & Sylvia headlined the inaugural Mariposa Folk Festival in Orillia, Ontario, along with the Travellers, a Jewish socialist outfit that was basically a Canadian knock-off of the Weavers. My claim to fame was designing the festival's poster, which won an art directors' award. That's the poster that hangs in my kitchen to this day.

That same year Pete Seeger played Massey Hall in Toronto and invited us onstage. It was our first performance in a big concert hall like that — Massey Hall is a very august and revered venue, and I'm sure we were scared stiff. I don't think we were playing very well back then, but it didn't matter. Folk was huge, and the shows were permeated by an incredible energy. It was like a runaway train. It was gonna go no matter what we did.

CHAPTER 4

New York

It was a rainy Manhattan autumn afternoon in 1962. I had borrowed our manager Albert Grossman's flat, somewhere in the east 50s, in order that I might write a song. I'd run into Bob Dylan the day before at my hangout, the Kettle of Fish in the Village, and Bob had sung me his latest. I want to say it was "Blowin' in the Wind," but memory does not serve me well in that regard. It could have been any one of his songs. At any rate, I'm listening and figuring, *Hey, how hard can this be? I know how the cold winds blow. I should give it a shot.* I had tried to write songs before, but it was all just incomplete scribbling.

In Albert's dingy flat I took out my Martin D28 and commenced strumming, drifting back out west to open country and my beautiful Greek girl from the Okanagan Valley. We had gone our separate ways, she to California and me to Toronto and New York City, and it was uncertain when or if we'd meet again (she hadn't yet married my friend Jack). The winds and seas were metaphors, though at the time I wouldn't have known a metaphor from a prairie gopher. I called the song "Four Strong Winds."

Sylvia and I had come to New York with our friend Joe Taylor, a Dixieland jazz freak who wrote for the *Toronto Star*. Joe had got caught up in the folk thing like everyone else, and being a really helpful guy with a car, in 1961 he offered to drive us down from Toronto.

We'd heard of this place called Gerde's Folk City and wanted to check it out. Gerde's was an open-mic folk club, only they didn't call them open mics in those days — they called them hootenannies or some damn thing. All the important folk promoters and managers were hanging around Gerde's listening for new talent, and all the up-and-comers would strut their stuff onstage at the Monday night hootenannies. If you got up and had something to say, they sure took notice of you.

Greenwich Village was a very competitive place by the time we arrived. Back in Toronto, if you could hold a guitar and pretend you were playing it, you had a gig. Not so in the Village. You needed the chops, and everyone was scrambling to improve as musicians. On Sundays Washington Square would fill up with Jewish kids playing bluegrass, practising standard songs such as "Michael, Row the Boat Ashore" on guitars and banjos. They'd form these little groups and play together for part of the afternoon before splitting off like amoebas and forming new groups to play with. That's not easy music to play, and if you could really play along, you were king.

Sylvia was also ambitious, aspiring to constantly improve as a singer and musician. I knew a lousy work ethic would get me nowhere in New York. For the first time in my life, I could smell success.

Sylvia had rented an apartment down on the Lower East Side, near the Williamsburg Bridge. I didn't have my own place in New York; I commuted back and forth to Toronto, chasing girls in both cities. I was always scuffling for a place to stay in New York. There were two hotels in the Village I stayed at; back then if you were half a day behind in your rent, they changed the lock on the door and you couldn't get your stuff. That happened to me a couple times. They didn't mess around.

Our social scene in the Village revolved around Gerde's, the Kettle of Fish and the Gaslight Café, a dingy little coffee-house directly downstairs from the Kettle of Fish. The Gaslight was run by Clarence Hood, an elderly Southerner from Mississippi, and his big, husky son, Sam. We played the Gaslight quite a bit and I liked Clarence and Sam a lot. Clarence always seemed a little out of place in New York. Looking at him and listening to his Southern accent, you'd have thought he was a hardware store owner in Georgia, not a coffee shop owner in Greenwich Village. He was a very courtly guy.

Peter, Paul and Mary were hanging around the clubs and coffeehouses with us, as were the singer-songwriters Tom Paxton and Fred Neil. We spent a lot of time with Dave Van Ronk, an established folksinger who had his own apartment (few people at the time owned their own flats). He was the social kingpin in the Village.

I also became friends with Ramblin' Jack Elliott, the original Brooklyn cowboy and a very influential figure in the Village. He had just returned from Europe, where he was a big star, when I met him. Jack had left home in Brooklyn pretty early, joining a travelling Wild West show when he was about fifteen. He was a product of the Woody Guthrie era, but like me he didn't buy into the socialism side of it. In

New York we spent a lot of time together at the old Hotel Earle on Washington Square. Both of us took great pride in our cowboy hats; Jack says I creased his hat for him by using a grapefruit to weigh it down in the sink. He returned the favour by teaching me his guitar method. His flat-pick style was very sophisticated, a blend of bluegrass and jazz. I think Jack influenced my guitar style more than anybody. We're still very good friends to this day.

But it was Dylan who got everybody's attention, because his style was so unconventional. When I met him after he'd come down out of Minnesota, he was loaded for bear. He knew exactly where he was going. He had focus. Of course it turned out he was a genius.

Truth be told, I didn't get Dylan at first. I didn't think he was that great a guitar player and I thought he was a terrible harmonica player. It took me quite a while to realize he was a great player — his style was simple yet powerful. When he started cranking out all those songs, you stood there amazed. But he was just one of the gang at first. He ran with Suze Rotolo, a good friend of Sylvia's.

In her memoir *A Freewheelin' Time*, Suze claims I was responsible for turning Dylan onto pot. I don't remember the details, but it may be true. I remember getting my dope from a cute Italian groupie from Chicago who took me by the ear. She was a pot smoker who dealt a little, and we ran together for a few months.

"You turned Bob Dylan onto pot," my singer-songwriter friend Tom Russell would later say. "Dylan turned on the Beatles. That makes you the *king*."

—

Ian & Sylvia. (JOHN ANDERSON)

Ian & Sylvia's hard work paid off quickly. After hearing us play around town a few times, Albert Grossman took us under his wing in 1962 and landed us a contract with Vanguard Records, a big label that had concentrated on classical music but was moving into folk.

Albert didn't have any money when we first met him, but he knew the jackpot was just around the corner. He was the architect who had put together Peter, Paul and Mary. He had also started managing Dylan right before he started working for us. Ramblin' Jack wanted Grossman to manage him too, but Albert wouldn't touch him because he could see that Jack was a wandering soul who wouldn't take direction. Albert was very territorial about his artists and his confrontational style rubbed certain people the wrong way, but he knew what he was doing, especially when it came to record contracts. He was a sharp guy.

After we signed the record deal, I knew I had to keep improving on the guitar. I learned a lot from John Herald, lead guitarist for the Greenbriar Boys. He played on our records and had a real melodic flair. John was one of the first urban folkies to develop that bluegrass style of hard, clean flat-picking — influenced by Gid Tanner and the Skillet Lickers, who were big in the 1920s. I would often head over to John's tiny flat in the Village to rehearse fairly intricate arrangements. I could never keep up. He was miles ahead of me, but I was playing decently.

Everyone in the folk scene started playing twelve-string guitars after the Rooftop Singers put out "Walk Right In" in 1962, the same year the first Ian & Sylvia record came out. Twelve-strings were the big fad, and I joined in for a couple years, playing a Gibson with a long peghead. But it was an unwieldy thing, hard to play and even harder to tune. Tuning that guitar was an art in itself and I didn't have the time to learn. Still, I managed to pull it off — until some kids stole my twelve-string while Sylvia was moving from one New York flat to another. They grabbed it right out of the moving van. That's the only guitar I've ever had stolen.

My flatpicking guitar style was a key part of the unique Ian & Sylvia sound. But Sylvia's concept of harmony was clearly the bedrock of our duo. I couldn't sing harmony — whenever I tried I would end up out of tune. So she sang harmony to my lead, and our voices created a unique style of folk interpretation, like nothing else around, as we performed Scots-Irish ballads and the occasional spiritual or French-Canadian song.

There was another secret to the Ian & Sylvia sound: Vanguard's recording studio, a musty three-storey ballroom inside a funky old hotel called the Manhattan Towers. That room had the magic, a completely natural quality of reverb. The room loved Ian & Sylvia's sound — particularly the vibrato in Sylvia's voice — and Ian & Sylvia loved the room. All Vanguard used was a German tape deck and a Neumann mic that hung down from the ceiling. Joan Baez and Odetta recorded there too. The records from that room are all incredible. It seemed you couldn't do anything wrong in that space. We had John on guitar and Bill Lee — Spike Lee's father — playing bass, and whenever we played in there, the guitars were just singing. The room enhanced and forgave.

When we weren't recording, we were performing. We did a three-week run in New York at the Blue Angel, a high-class nightclub on East 55th Street for emerging stars, with Barbra Streisand, who was an unknown at the time. She did a pretty good job but we struggled every night, as I recall. I didn't know how to put on a show back then. I wasn't extroverted on stage and didn't know anything about the aesthetics of performing — where to place songs in the set list and how to present them. It would take a long time for me to learn.

The Village was its own little kingdom, its own insular world, and it took me a while to figure out that Ian & Sylvia were getting big. I clued in when we started playing at this Washington, D.C., club called the Cellar Door, a tiny, suffocatingly hot place that became very influential in the folk circuit. It had no air conditioning and no monitors and seated only about 140 people, every one of them soaking wet. We packed the place with college kids every single time.

The second time we played the Cellar Door, Vanguard had a brain flash — which was unusual for that label — and arranged for us to have a Saturday album-signing party. At the signing our fans mobbed us as if we were stars. That was my first inkling that we were huge. From that one club we got booked at the Ivy League schools, as well as clubs in California such as the Golden Bear and the hungry i. All that meant we were making big money, something neither Sylvia nor I had experienced before.

After we put out the albums *Four Strong Winds* and *Northern Journey* in 1964, Ian & Sylvia were really hot. We toured the U.K., played the Newport Folk Festival and even sold out Carnegie Hall. Robert Shelton, a music critic for the *New York Times*, raved that Ian & Sylvia were "well equipped to outrun any temporary decline of interest in folk music" and that we had "one of the finest blends of male and female voices in the folk revival."

Something else happened in 1964 that would affect Ian & Sylvia — and the rest of the folkies — in a big way. A British band called the Beatles played the *Ed Sullivan Show* in February, and pretty soon rock and roll was hitting America like a tsunami. I remember driving to a gig in New Jersey with Sylvia, our guitarist Monte Dunn and bass player Felix Pappalardi. We were listening to the radio and this song started playing: *She loves you, yeah, yeah, yeah* . . . It was a

Our publicity still. (COURTESY IAN TYSON)

new, appealing sound, and the guys loved it. I thought the lyrics were dumb but I loved the music too, especially the harmony. Sylvia was less sure about it. Maybe she sensed that these British up-and-comers were going to be our downfall. Sure enough, Monte and Felix eventually left us to join or form their own Beatlesque rock bands.

Sylvia and I, meanwhile, grew increasingly fond of each other. I had been running with lots of girls and Sylvia had her fair share of boyfriends, but over time Ian & Sylvia evolved into something more than music. We got married on June 26, 1964, at Toronto's St. Thomas's Anglican Church on Huron Street. Afterwards we moved into a big house in the Rosedale area of Toronto.

While our affection for one another was very real, the truth is that Sylvia and I had completely different interests. Had we not been inextricably bonded by our music careers, we probably would not have married — but if we hadn't married, there would have been no Clay Tyson.

Sylvia was an urban person through and through. I liked the bright lights of New York and Toronto too, but I needed to get out of the city on a regular basis. I wanted to be around horses and cattle again. Ontario had a small-town rodeo circuit, and sure enough, I got hooked back into riding and roping calves.

In 1965 I came up with a plan to spend more time outside the city: I'd buy a bit of land. That year I went with my friend Jake Banky to look at a cattle farm near Bowmanville, Ontario, and ended up buying the place, even though I didn't have a clue how to run a farm. I got horses and a nice little herd of Hereford cows, and I hired this handy old guy, Dick Weirmer, to take care of it all.

Going to Bowmanville was like stepping into a time capsule. It wasn't far from Toronto, but driving those fifty miles you'd go back a hundred years. Old men who lived in big brick farmhouses would drive around in horses and buggies — not to be colourful, but just because that's what they did.

I was haying on the farm the day Clay was born in June 1966. It was a complicated birth ending in a C-section, and he'd been born by the time I arrived at the hospital. It sounds strange, but I always think of Clay in horse-breeding terms. He's almost a fifty-fifty cross: he looks like his mother and he looks like me. He's got red hair, which comes from Sylvia's side. But he's got my dark eyebrows and eyes and he's built like me. His way of dealing with the world came from us both too; that's where I really see the cross. His love of conversation and debate comes from his mom, but, like his old man, he can be irascible on occasion.

After Clay was born we'd always take him along on tour with help from Hazel, his faithful Jamaican nanny. Hazel played a big role in raising Clay on the road, an arrangement we never had any trouble with until Christmas Day, 1967. We were scheduled to fly to California for four weeks of gigs at the Golden Bear in Huntington Beach and the Troubadour in L.A. Hazel was going to come along, as always, but this time the American border officers at the Toronto airport refused to let her fly into the U.S. Poor Hazel didn't understand why she was being denied — she probably didn't have the necessary visa — and the experience made her very distraught. The thought of playing a month of gigs without Hazel's help was upsetting for Sylvia too. She knew it would be exhausting, since Clay was regularly waking up a few times each night. We had little choice, though, so we boarded the plane for L.A. while Hazel stayed behind.

After we arrived, we rented an apartment at Huntington Beach. Sure enough, after playing a few gigs at the Golden Bear and having to wake up with Clay at night and walk him around the parking lot to calm him down, Sylvia snapped. She couldn't operate on so little sleep. She came back to the apartment one day and started hollering at me — which was very unlike her — so right away I scooped up little Clay and took him to the beach. For the next couple of weeks Clay and I spent our days on the beach hanging out with my buddies from the folk clubs and picking kelp off the sand. The weather was perfect. Sylvia probably worried about what we were doing down there, but we were just hanging out. Clay was a well-behaved little guy.

California felt very innocent back then. Sylvia and I used to visit this folk DJ up near Long Beach who pretty much embodied the California ethos. His big old potbelly hung over his cut-off shorts, his beard had four days' growth and he had sand on his feet. It was that kind of existence in California back then, laid back and carefree. I don't remember any hassles.

It was the height of the sixties, though, and many of the people making money in music back then did a lot of psychedelics and other heavy drugs. During that California trip my guitar player, Monte Dunn, rented the apartment next to ours. He stayed there with another rounder musician, Tim Hardin. Both of them were heavily into drugs. We wouldn't see them at all during the day. They were like slugs under a log, refusing to stick their faces out into the sunlight.

Tim eventually died of a heroin overdose when he was thirty-nine. LSD wrecked a lot of musicians too. I took acid a few times and liked it, but when I came down I could tell that my motor had been severely tried. I knew it could be really dangerous, and I never became a regular user.

As time went on and opposition to the Vietnam War intensified, folk got more and more politicized — and we suffered because of that. Ian & Sylvia had always been relatively apolitical. We had toured a bit with Lady Bird Johnson and Faron Young in 1964 as part of Lyndon Johnson's re-election campaign, but for the most part we did our best to steer clear of politics.

Sylvia felt that protest music made for good protest but bad music. I felt similarly. I never went along with the Woody Guthrie socialism and union stuff. It just didn't resonate with me. I couldn't get my head around "This Land Is Your Land" because I knew loggers, cowboys and fishermen, and not many of them were socialists. When I worked on the pipeline with Jack Bruce after art school, I witnessed corrupt union politics firsthand and saw how the union tended to screw things up.

While American draft dodgers were fleeing north to Canada, I registered for the draft in the U.S. — my green card made it compulsory for me to do so. I would have gone to Vietnam, as some of my buddies did, but I was deemed 4-F (unfit for military service) because of my bum knee that I blew out in boarding school. I was goddamn lucky I didn't end up there, because I'd probably have gotten my head blown off.

As time went on, anybody with half a brain — myself

included — realized the war was a terrible mistake. But the farm boys from Oklahoma didn't know that, and when they got over there it was too late. A lot of them didn't come back. The ones who did return were very changed. I remember seeing boys on leave when my band played Osaka, Japan, in 1970, and they looked like ghosts in their cheap civilian suits. That's a haunting memory.

It's the screwed-up American way: go marching in, guns blazing, and after three weeks not only is the conflict not over, it hasn't even begun. It happens over and over. The U.S. is doing the same thing today — still hasn't learned anything.

But in the 1960s there was no way I could jump on the protest bandwagon. People like Country Joe and the Fish wanted everything to be free, with no responsibility. They wanted bread and circuses like the Romans. They were totally full of shit and people went along with it. I couldn't. I remember playing some kind of environment concert down in Philadelphia, where all these kids sat around congratulating themselves on how wonderful they were. They went on to trash the whole place. After the concert the park was absolutely filthy. Those kids shat on everything — and this was supposed to be about the environment. To me the popular politics of the day just didn't add up.

People like to talk about the folk revival as an "era." I don't know if three years can be an era, but that's basically what it was — at least, that's what it was for Ian & Sylvia. We did three or maybe four very influential records, and that's it. As the decade wore on, the hipsters started to ignore us. We got no respect in the New York milieu anymore. We used to be California darlings, but now we couldn't get arrested there if we wanted to. Many came to consider us a schlock act. We still had our faithful adherents, but the bloom was off the rose. Another tectonic shift in music and culture was underway, and we weren't part of it.

By the late 1960s Vanguard had moved drums into the room in Manhattan Towers. You could not put drums in that room and keep its celestial vocal sound. But rock and roll was taking over, so eventually we had to have drums like everyone else. Then Albert landed us a deal with MGM, and we recorded our last few Ian & Sylvia albums in Nashville. In the late 1960s all the folkies, including Dylan and Joan Baez, were recording in Nashville.

Nashville had great session players but the city itself turned out to be a disappointment when we arrived there in 1967 to record *Lovin' Sound*. We were staying at the Capitol Park Inn downtown, and we couldn't find anyplace to eat dinner after seven o'clock at night. It's a sophisticated place now, but back then Nashville was just a farm town where all the Baptist literature got published. The music scene was pretty underground.

Despite Nashville's dullness we recorded some fine records there, experimenting with a more country-rock sound. In 1968 we recorded *Full Circle* at Bradley's Barn, a legendary studio just outside the city, where we met great Nashville players such as Kenny Buttrey and Norbert Putnam. They formed the rhythm section on *Full Circle*. We encouraged our players to do long instrumental solos, and David Rea, our lead guitarist, was obviously very keen on that. *Full*

Circle was a good record, one of Ian & Sylvia's best, though it didn't make the charts.

In 1969 we played the *Johnny Cash Show* at Nashville's Ryman Auditorium. It felt like 104 degrees in there and there was no air conditioning. John introduced us as a duo from "the land of the maple and the Douglas fir" and paid our songwriting a fine compliment: "When I like a piece of music that I hear, that's when I say, 'I wish I'd written that.' In the case of the people you're about to meet, I've said those words many, many times concerning their songs." John's genuineness really came through on that show. I admired him very much. We had recorded a couple of his songs — "Come in Stranger" and "Big River" — and John liked me and admired my work too. He thought "Red Velvet" was a huge song, though he never got around to cutting it. He eventually did a version of "Four Strong Winds" instead.

We didn't play Woodstock in 1969. The common myth is that if you didn't play Woodstock you weren't happening, but a lot of us didn't play it. Joni Mitchell didn't play Woodstock — and she wrote the biggest song about it.

Still, it was undeniable: Ian & Sylvia had been a fad. Albert Grossman started focusing less on us and more on Dylan and new up-and-comers. He bought a place in Woodstock, which became the hub of his empire. The Band went there to work on their seminal self-titled album and became the focus of the Grossman organization, second only to Dylan — and of course he merged them. Throughout all of this we got short shrift.

It all hit my ego pretty hard. I didn't like going from being a top-of-the-pile folk duo to a discredited schlock act, from prince and princess of the whole thing to nothing. I got pretty angry about it. Around 1970 Sylvia and I went to see the Flying Burrito Brothers at a little joint in Manhattan. They were loud and out of tune, but we could see that they were going somewhere, and I was stewing because I thought we were much better than they were. I got drunk; I remember yelling at Sylvia as we left the club.

All this was hard on her too. Sylvia's ego wasn't as easily bruised as mine, and she was way more even-tempered than me. I don't think she was upset about the Beatles or the Burritos or any of it. I was angry because we had fallen out of fashion — and I didn't know what to do about it.

I kept drifting into country rock and getting to know more of the Nashville players. I really liked the Waylon-and-Willie movement and wanted to be part of that, but I never was. I was a bluegrass freak too. But the guitar playing was very demanding and difficult. Had I been able to play well enough, I probably would have ended up as a bluegrass musician.

Instead I formed a country-rock band called Great Speckled Bird, named after the Roy Acuff song of the same name. Sylvia, Amos Garrett (guitar), Buddy Cage (steel guitar), Jim Colegrove (bass), N.D. Smart (drums) and David Wilcox (guitar) were all part of the band at various times.

We recorded our only album in 1970. *Great Speckled Bird* is a very good record, and today it's recognized as such, but we didn't know how to reproduce that rock sound live. In the studio the engineers controlled the electronics, but onstage I didn't have their help with my electric guitar. The other guys struggled with the tech too.

Great Speckled Bird, from left: N.D. Smart, Buddy Cage, me, Sylvia, David Wilcox and Jim Colegrove. (DON NEWLANDS)

In 1970 we played the Festival Express, the Canadian cross-country train tour, where we did a lot of jamming with Jerry Garcia and the Grateful Dead and The Band. Jerry was a real social guy who sure knew how to keep those jams going. There was a lot of dope smoking and drinking on the train — everyone had a cigarette hanging out of his or her mouth, and Janis Joplin drank everyone under the table — but the jams were really quite good.

The tour became a big political mess after the dopers and hippies tried to take over the event in Toronto and force us and the rest of the artists to do our concerts for free. I wasn't interested in that at all. The press poured gasoline all over the situation, aiding and abetting the hippies' cause, and then sanctimoniously claimed they weren't taking sides. Thankfully Kenny Walker, the promoter, never backed down. He told the hippies to eff off, which was the right thing to do.

I broke my hand on some knucklehead's noggin when the train stopped in Calgary in July. My drummer, N.D. Smart, had started kibitzing with these farm boys who'd pulled up to a stop sign beside us. It escalated after we pulled over in front of the Cecil Hotel, on the east side of downtown. Both sides started throwing punches. The other guys backed down only when they realized who I was, but by then I had busted my left hand — a bit of a problem, since I had to play. I've always had a temper.

We kept touring the U.S. and Canada, but the colleges we'd played as Ian & Sylvia hated us when we showed up with Great Speckled Bird. There was one exception: Berkley. They loved the band. But the Ivy League schools we'd famously played as a duo couldn't handle the change from acoustic folk to country rock. It was like Bob Dylan plugging in, albeit on a much lesser scale.

The sound systems weren't very good in those days, which didn't help. There was absolutely no balancing of monitors. Musicians live by monitors — without them, we can't play good music — but we didn't have the quality technology we have today. It was very primitive. The rock bands really did everyone a favour by blowing out all those crappy Shure sound systems. They're all gone now, and good riddance. The Japanese saw the market potential and they started making quality equipment.

The real problem in Great Speckled Bird was that I didn't

know how to be a bandleader. When I worked with Sylvia alone, since she loved me and was an old-fashioned girl, she pretty much did what I told her to do. But when I formed a band with four or five other guys, it was a completely different story.

This was an unruly bunch. Being on time didn't mean anything to them. On the road you've got to be a road warrior, you've got to stand and be counted. If you're supposed to be at the bus at a certain time, you be there at that time — not ten minutes late. These guys all thought otherwise. They looked at our tours as a laissez-faire communal dope-smoking party. You can't run a band like that.

The guys were just immature and so was I. Since then I've learned some crucial life lessons about being a bandleader. You've got to be completely honest and consistent day in and day out. Your word has got to be law and your word has to be good, all the time. If you take the easy way out and bend the truth, even over a silly detail like scheduling on the road, it'll come back to bite you on the ass. The band members expect you to be above reproach, even when they're not.

If one of the band members tries it on with you, you call his bluff right away. By the time I caught on to all this, Great Speckled Bird was long gone. Bands are as good as their weakest link, but in the trio I play with now (Gord Maxwell on bass and Lee Worden on guitar), there is no weak link. Maybe I'm skewed in my opinion, but I think the western boys are more solid, more responsible — especially if they're country boys.

All these lessons I learned about being a bandleader apply to riding horses too. You need consistency and you can't lose your temper. You need to be able to read things that are coming up. And with both musicians and horses, you lead by example.

Despite my failings as a bandleader, Great Speckled Bird broke up only when Jesse Winchester's people rustled my guys. I don't think Jesse himself could have engineered it, but his people came to the Montreal hotel where we were playing. A few days later the majority of my band was out the door.

Time heals and people eventually grow up. That's where patience comes in. All of us Great Speckled Bird guys are pretty good friends after all these years.

CHAPTER 5

Horses

By the time Great Speckled Bird broke up in the early 1970s, I was doing a weekly half-hour country music show out of Toronto. The show had originally been called *Nashville North*, but in the second year CFTO-TV changed the name to the *Ian Tyson Show*. I'd open each episode with a song with the band (the remnants of Great Speckled Bird) and then we'd bring on the guests, singers such as Willie Nelson, Faron Young, Johnny Rodriguez, Mel Tillis, Dolly Parton and Conway Twitty.

While Sylvia sang on some of the episodes, both the station and I were kind of squeezing her out. I wanted to learn how to sing solo country music. I wasn't sure if I could handle it or not and I figured the show would be a test for that. My goal was to find a good generic country music style — a radio-friendly style — and there was no way I could do that in the context of our duo. The duet is a pretty restrictive format because you always have to blend and there's little room for extemporaneous vocals. You're always

With Conway Twitty on The Ian Tyson Show. (COURTESY IAN TYSON)

throwing your voice up against the other voice to get that clean harmony sound. That's true of all duos — not only Ian & Sylvia, but also Simon and Garfunkel, the Everly Brothers and so on.

It was important for me to go beyond Ian & Sylvia, and the station wasn't interested in belabouring the duo sound either. It was time for Ian & Sylvia to end, but the move would strain our marriage. I'm sure Sylvia was offended, though at the time it seemed that she took it all in stride. Or maybe that was me just being oblivious.

As it turned out, I handled the solo work on the show

just fine. My band rehearsed constantly; we were hungry and worked hard, and we garnered great ratings. I didn't have my true vocal style down yet — that would come later, in the cowboy recordings — but we knew how to play country music. We had focus.

I put out my first solo album, *Ol' Eon*, on A&M Records in 1973. The only reason I was on A&M was because of Albert Grossman's power. To this day I think *Ol' Eon* is a good record, but it didn't get much attention. Nobody would give it a break. I couldn't find that breakthrough song that gives a musician an identity. That's how the industry worked back then, and still works to this day — you need the big song. Johnny Cash had "I Walk the Line." Johnny Rodriguez had "Pass Me By." Marty Robbins had "El Paso." And I just couldn't find that Ian Tyson song.

Canada had decided that its country hero was going to be Stompin' Tom Connors, who won the Juno award for best country male vocalist every year from 1971 to 1975. He obviously struck a chord with certain Canadians, but I didn't identify with his music. (As well, I thought the Toronto crowd's acceptance of his work was pretty condescending and patronizing. To me it seemed that they regarded Connors's material as hick music.) I was pretty bitter about Stompin' Tom's popularity at the time. He had as much right to be successful in show business as anybody, but I didn't have the maturity to deal with other people's success.

There's a lot to be said for hanging in there when you're not getting the recognition you think you deserve. Some musicians, like Jack Elliott, do that effortlessly, soldiering on through different fads and "eras" without any anger,

Solo. (COURTESY IAN TYSON)

focusing on perfecting their art. That perseverance usually pays off. But I didn't get that at the time. *Why the hell do I have to hang in there?* I wondered. I wanted recognition *now*.

I was also jealous of Gordon Lightfoot's success. I'd helped him a lot when he was scuffling to get established in Toronto, and Ian & Sylvia had recorded a couple of his songs ("Early Morning Rain" and "For Loving Me") when we were hot in the mid-1960s. I talked him up to Albert Grossman's partner, John Court, who came up to Toronto and checked Gordon out, and they signed a contract. But it seemed that once Gordon became successful, he treated his old friends like unnecessary burdens from the past. He had all those hits in the 1970s, and I always felt he should have repaid the personal debt by cutting one of my tunes. Eventually, in the 1990s, he did cover one of my old Ian & Sylvia songs, "Red Velvet" — the song Johnny Cash was also a great fan of.

Sylvia and I kept drifting apart. We had very different ideas about how we wanted to live. When I wasn't recording the TV show, I spent most of my time at the farm. She preferred Rosedale. Our musical careers had brought and held us together, but now that Ian & Sylvia was finished, our marriage slowly dissolved. We spent less and less time together even though we were technically still married.

Another woman entered my life as this was all going down. I was playing an old club in Montreal with the TV band when Katie Malloch came down to check us out. I think she was stringing for the CBC at the time — she would go on to host a variety of successful CBC shows — and we fell hard for each other. Katie thought it was very romantic to be running around with a cowboy in Montreal. I'd go visit her there and she would come down to my farm when she could. For some reason my little bay mare took an instant dislike to Katie and bucked her off, breaking her wrist.

Clay also visited me regularly at the cattle farm. He did well out there. Even as a boy, Clay had a real aptitude around livestock. Clay knew about Katie — sometimes they were at the farm at the same time — but it's hard to say what he felt about our affair back then. I wasn't being very sensitive about the whole thing, that's for sure.

Katie and I liked each other a lot, and eventually I told Sylvia. That was the breaking point. Sylvia could accept a lot of things but she couldn't accept that. I don't blame her.

Clay was eight or nine when we split in 1975. After we separated he lived with his mother, attending a Rosedale school for kids of well-to-do businesspeople and professionals. Being a shy kid, Clay had trouble fitting in. He struggled to pay attention in class, just as I had.

It was during this time of marital drifting and divorce that I became a serious horseman. I wish I could say it happened in cow country in the middle of Wyoming, but it happened in eastern Canada. A couple cowboys I rodeoed with, Jim McKay and Don Waugh, worked for Walter Hellyer, a farmer down near Waterford, Ontario. Walter and his family ran one of the first commercially successful ginseng operations in North America, but they also ran cattle and raised horses. Hellyer was very interested in quarter horses. By the time I met him, he'd started bringing up horses from

Texas — mostly old-style cowboy horses that came from the stud Hollywood Gold.

Jim and Don told me to get down to Hellyer's place and ride these cutting horses. I had never ridden a cutting horse before, and I decided to give it a shot. Cutting has a long tradition in the West. After the American Civil War, when Texas cowman Charles Goodnight became the first man to drive cattle from Texas to Colorado, the Anglo cowboy was inventing himself on the job. There were no fences back then, and cattle from different owners mingled together on the open range. Charlie and the other cowboys would make sweeps of the country to gather huge herds for the drive. Then, if they had the time as they went up the trail, they would cut out the different brands and the owners would drive them back to their home range. (And if Charlie ended up driving somebody else's cattle to Colorado, he'd even out the ledger with the owner when he got back, paying or trading for the cattle.)

Cowboys being cowboys, cutting cows from the herd quickly became competitive — not only for the riders but for the horses too. Those old punchers didn't have the specially bred athletic horses we have now, nor did they have the perfectly manicured arenas with five or six inches of dirt to keep the horses from breaking their legs. The ponies in the old days had to do it among the cactus and the rocks and everything else.

In cutting it's hard to know where the horse leaves off and the rider takes over. "You must learn to ride in a way that does not drag at the motion of a horse," wrote my friend Thomas McGuane in a 1991 *Sports Illustrated* story on cutting. "The body language between you and the horse must be bright and clear." In contests you're not allowed to rein the horse, so all the cuing has to be done with your legs and spurs. You've got to stay centred on the saddle, hook your fingers under the saddle pad and keep them there until you quit the cow. McGuane again: "The herd instinct of cattle is tremendously strong, and to drive out an individual cow and hold her against this tidal force, a horse must act with knowledge, physical skill and precision. Otherwise, the cow escapes and returns to a thoroughly upset herd."

When the horse made those first big moves to cut the cow from the herd at Hellyer's farm, the G-force gave me a rush — a wonderful thrill I've felt every time I've ridden a cutting horse since. It's unavoidable. The combination of explosive power and fluid movement becomes addictive very quickly. This was a hell of a lot better than goofing around at B.C. rodeos.

Hellyer took a liking to me and lined me up with my first cutting horse, Deljay's Pistol, a gelding from Ohio that belonged to Dr. Leroy Hyman, another famous eastern cutting-horse breeder and cowboy. Deljay's Pistol was a very kind horse; when I took him on the Ontario cutting-horse circuit, he'd overcome all my mistakes and still win us some prize money. And when I started winning cash, I was really hooked.

For whatever reason, Hellyer was very anxious for me to start breeding good horses myself. He'd bought four brood-mares in the early 1970s from Dr. and Mrs. Stephen Jensen of the Double J Ranch in California. These weren't just any mares, however. They were daughters of Doc Bar, a revolutionary stallion that was rewriting the book on the breeding of cutting horses. For a bargain price Hellyer sold me one of those daughters, a big buckskin broodmare named Doc's Able Mable — a well-travelled, placid old gal foaled in 1965 in California.

Having a horse with Doc Bar blood was a very big deal in the 1970s. Foaled in Arizona in 1956, Doc Bar was bred for the track, but it turned out he couldn't outrun a fat man, earning just ninety-five dollars in four races. The little chestnut stud had other qualities, however. He was pretty as a picture; somebody once said he looked like "a perfect little watch fob." Doc Bar's perfect conformation won him a total of nine halter-horse grand championships, completely changing the ideal for the halter industry.

Doc Bar was just getting started. A prescient horseman named Charlie Araujo then turned him into a phenomenal success as a breeding horse. Charlie was a mystic who could look right inside a horse's head, almost as if he had a built-in MRI. Somehow he knew that if he crossed Doc Bar with the Jensens' Poco Tivio mares, he'd really have something. How exactly he knew this remains a mystery, but the stars were definitely aligned when the horse gods brought Doc Bar and Charlie together. Charlie's prediction was bang on. Doc Bar had perfect conformation and prepotency — the ability to deliver all his traits to his progeny — and I was very fortunate to get one of his daughters.

When I got Doc's Able Mable in the 1970s, a cutting broodmare spent many long days on the road, much like a musician. The American Quarter Horse Association hadn't yet ordained the shipping of frozen semen by FedEx, which meant the mare had to make the long journey to the stud — and that usually meant Texas. So I took Doc's Able Mable to Buster Welch, the greatest cutting-horse trainer of them all. (In addition to being an exceptional rider and breeder, Buster pioneered the use of the round pen for training cutting horses and helped start the National Cutting Horse Association futurity in Fort Worth, Texas — an annual December cutting competition for three-year-old horses that haven't been shown previously.)

Buster bred Doc's Able Mable to his horse, a rising star named Mr. San Peppy. After running with Mr. San Peppy for a year, Mable was still open (not in foal). Finally Buster called me to announce that she'd caught, and it was back on the road for the mare — "uphill from Texas," as the old drovers used to say, to Ontario. On February 10, 1975, Mabel foaled out a little yellow colt. I named him Doc's Summer Wages.

As a yearling, Doc's Summer Wages — or Yeller, as I called him — wasn't much to look at. He was small and clay-bank yellow, just a colt. When he turned two, I stepped up on him, and within five seconds I was sitting on the ground with my batwing chaps over my shoulders like an errant knight's cape. He didn't buck; he just faded out from underneath me so fast he left me standing in midair.

For a long time I had ridden horses like my old man: get on and go. But now I was starting to move beyond that, learning real respect for a horse's mind. The horse seems to know he's a servant of man, and he somehow understands that, by moving with endurance and speed, he can enable man to do certain things.

The journey to the mind and soul of a horse is a long one — never-ending, perhaps. When you spend all your time with horses, you want to understand them fully. But you can't, and that's the mystery that fascinates us. You can go as far as legendary horsemen like Buster Welch, and still you'll never fully arrive. It's challenging to go even that far, as top horsemen have always been very guarded about their knowledge. Buster was one of the exceptions. Catch him in the right mood and he'd share a bit. But horsemen like cutting legend Shorty Freeman didn't say a thing. It just wasn't part of what they did. The only way to learn from those guys was by observation. There's a lot of logic to that, because there are no shortcuts with horses. You have to put in the time.

I've heard people say that horses are stupid, but they're not. They're clearly capable of loyalty and affection to humans. I've had two cowboys tell me that they suffered a heart attack, passed out and awakened to find their mount standing over them, as if on guard. But as herd animals of the savannah, horses are wired differently than we are. Too often people expect human-style rational behaviour from the horse. That can never be. For them, self-preservation comes first. Evolution has taught them that flight is their first survival option. The second one is fight.

Horses are like people: there are dumb ones and there are smart ones. Get the halter on and saddle them for a job, and you can sense their excitement. I've seen it so many times. Set out to herd cattle with a good horse and he'll think the work is wonderful, even though you might not be able to catch him in the morning. Just like people, horses enjoy being assholes occasionally. They're full of pride, and when they're working well, they know it.

—

I quit the *Ian Tyson Show* in 1975—I was forty-one—as cutting horses were taking up more of my time and attention. I wanted to keep both playing music and cutting, but I knew if I hung on the station would eventually discard me. I wanted to walk while the show was on top.

To my surprise, after the show ended I couldn't get music work in Ontario. I went to Nashville to get my act together musically but didn't find success there either. It was the start of that big-hat, beer-drinking period down there. A lot of guys were writing incredibly stupid country songs, and they'd become hits. That scene didn't interest me at all.

In Nashville I cut some decent demos that didn't go anywhere. I think the Nashville producer types saw through me — saw that I probably wouldn't commit and be the indentured servant type of artist they wanted in those days. They wanted you to get on the tour bus and stay there. And the more success you got, the harder they were on you. They made you a slave, basically. I've heard that industry people still say, "Ian won't take direction." In my mind that translates into "Ian won't stay on the damn bus for 300 days a year."

One guy who got away with getting off that hamster wheel was George Strait. He toured a lot but he also had his ranch. He broke that old pattern where you just worked all the time and if you didn't agree to it, the industry people brushed you off. That's what I like to think my problem was back then — as opposed to lack of talent.

I realized I had to find my way somewhere outside the country market. Nashville has a cool eclectic musical underground, but for the most part it's become a factory for the junk on country radio. As a western singer, you have to find another route. (That used to bother me, but when you've been around as long as I have, you learn to roll with it.)

So I headed back to my farm in Canada and conjured a plan to move to Texas, where land was cheap. I wanted to live in the West. I've always said it's hard to be a cowboy in Ontario, and it's true. Lots of guys try it, but it lacks authenticity somehow. Ultimately I couldn't relate to the life and culture there. It's perfect for some people, but not for me.

Besides, I was having trouble with a neighbour who had opened a landfill right beside my place at a time when hardly any environmental laws were enforced in the area. A wannabe cowboy friend of mine, Frank Watts, worked as an on-again, off-again realtor. "I think we can sell him your place if you want," he told me.

"Think so? Because I'd like to get out of here."

I was still running with Katie Malloch, but that was starting to unravel too. The distance between Montreal and southern Ontario made it hard to carry on the relationship. So there wasn't much left for me in eastern Canada anymore.

But my Texas ambitions hit a snag, all because of a free-spirit benefit concert of some kind that I'd played in Montreal a few years prior. During the show I'd left my guitar case open on the stage, and a few fans tossed joints into the case. The airline lost my guitar and it ended up in Jamaica or the Bahamas or some damn place, joints and all. The guitar made it back to Toronto a couple days later, but it arrived with two big, burly plainclothes Mounties. They had opened the case and discovered the pot, and they followed up by getting a warrant and searching my house, where they found some hashish.

The situation devolved into theatre of the absurd. I didn't smoke a lot of dope; I did it as a social thing, but that's it. I didn't go nuts the way so many people did back then. But those asshole Mounties decided they were going to get me regardless. I had to go to court, where I got a conditional discharge. Strangely, the incident got hardly any press attention.

Because of the conditional discharge, my criminal record in Canada was clean, but I was still guilty in the eyes of the FBI, who promptly jerked my green card. And there was no way I could get myself out of their computers. It caused me all kinds of trouble when I tried crossing the border. If I crossed as a cowboy with my horse trailer, I could always get into the U.S. without problems — the border guys cut cowboys slack for some reason. But if I went with a guitar, the border officers would hassle me no end and sometimes even turn me back. That happened for many years until I got some kind of border ID card in the mail that eliminated the problem.

I'm no fan of the U.S.–Canadian border — what the old-time Natives called the "Medicine Line." It's just an arbitrary line that follows no river, mountain range or natural boundary of any kind. It's a political invention that ignores the rhythms of nature and the flow of the seasons. The cowboy culture has always ignored that arbitrary line as much as possible, but increasingly we're forced to live with it. One of my neighbours has stopped going to weekend horse shows in Montana because crossing the border is too much of a hassle. That's not good for the horse industry at all. And the ranchers here in Alberta suffered greatly when the U.S. shut the border to Canadian beef a few years back. BSE (most people know it as "mad cow disease") sure as hell doesn't recognize a border, no matter how the politicos spin it.

Regardless of my strong opinions about the Medicine Line, I couldn't move to Texas without a green card. So I decided to head west to Alberta instead.

I got the idea of moving to Alberta when my band and I played Calgary in the mid-1970s, doing a week of gigs at Ranchman's, the local honky-tonk — a place I'd come to know very well. We stayed at the Carriage House Inn on Macleod Trail, and I remember looking out the window of my sixth-floor room and witnessing this incredible sunset. The purple hills and rose-coloured Rockies were very dramatic, reminiscent of the paintings of Charlie Russell. I stood in awe of that sunset and thought, *I'd kind of like to live here.* The horse industry in southern Alberta wasn't very big back then, but I could see it was growing.

In 1978 I loaded up the horse trailer and drove west with my buddy Frank. We headed for a ranch at Pincher Creek, about 140 miles south of Calgary, where I knew the foreman, Alan Young. I had met Alan in the late 1960s at a competitive trail ride in the Cypress Hills; we had both been recruited as judges. He recognized me as a kindred spirit right away, and I recognized him right back. Youthful and athletic, he seemed like a carefree, upbeat cowboy. We hit it off in the Cypress Hills and partied together for most of the week.

Alan was a quintessential westerner, an unforgettable character with a reputation for toughness. He was like one of the old forest rangers in those western American towns

My friend, Alan Young, foreman of the Pincher Creek ranch.

where they picked the toughest guy in town to be in charge. Alan loved being around people, but his one quality that didn't quite jibe with the western toughness was that he loved to hang with people who were higher than him on the social scale. When I was doing the TV show in Toronto, he'd come visit once in a while and would always want to hang out with movie stars, wealthy people and musicians.

Eventually Alan became the foreman of a large Pincher Creek ranch owned by Parisian entrepreneurs. "Come on out," he suggested. "We'll have a party that will continue here 24/7." Alan was married now and had kids, but he still liked to party hard.

Moving to an Alberta ranch sounded like a good idea to me. My middle-age crazies were kicking in. I was forty-four but wanted to be twenty-two again, chasing girls, horses and cows.

Moving my stuff out to Pincher Creek took a couple of trips, and Frank helped out a lot, hauling my furniture — including the big wooden table I still use for writing — to a little creekside cabin on the ranch. At Pincher I was all cowboy, training horses, chewing Copenhagen and having girls visit me in my tiny cabin. I was really living the life.

Clay, who was eleven or twelve, came out to visit a few times, and he was pretty upset when he saw me with my Alberta girlfriends. He was a vulnerable kid, loyal to his mother, and I was pretty insensitive to what he was going through. But Clay could ride steers and he got along real well with my stud, so I let him ride the stud at a show. As I recall, he won a couple hundred bucks and a pair of spurs — and of course he was very happy about that. He was a good little rider. He got a painful rope burn on his hand during one visit, but I think that was the only time he got hurt. He was a brave soul and I enjoyed having him out there.

At Pincher, whether Clay was visiting or not, we still partied, just as Alan had promised — especially when the Parisians were around. Alan in particular smoked like a chimney and drank a lot of whiskey. Ever aware of his obligation to entertain, he was always doing the cowboy shtick, always thinking of his next one-liner. Whenever he met somebody at a party, he'd ask, "Howdoyalikeitoutwest?" He'd get funny looks, but those of us who knew Alan got a kick out of it. He'd use stock one-liners like that over and over until we knew them all by heart.

When it came to horses, though, Alan was just like my old man — make 'em do it. Horses were tools to be used, and used hard. He had tried rodeoing a bit, with mixed results. "I never had much of a lick on the saddle broncs," he told me once, making reference to his spurring. It was a hard thing for him to admit. He recalled working for a Texan on an old-style desert ranch in southern Alberta years earlier. "I'd get twenty miles into the desert and I'd be terrified that I'd get bucked off and get stranded out there and have to walk back. I never learned to loosen up. I wouldn't get bucked off, but I wouldn't win anything either."

We had a lot of fun at Pincher. At the start of the summer of 1978, a wise old cowman from Lethbridge, George Brooks, wanted to run yearlings on the ranch (he was a friend of Alan's). I liked George right away — he's seventeen years older than me, so I started calling him Uncle George — and we formed an old-fashioned handshake partnership. Uncle George, a banker and I paid the ranch to summer the steers, with the idea of making a bunch of money down the road. We ran about 1,800 yearlings — and we got rustled. I don't know exactly who was behind it, but some of the branded cattle ended up on the nearby Peigan reserve, Brocket. In any case, we still made money from the deal.

Earlier in 1978 I had sent Doc's Summer Wages to Bill Freeman, son of cutting legend Shorty Freeman, for training. Bill was another rising star in the cutting world, and when I visited him and Yeller in Missouri that summer, I was amazed at the latter's transformation. He had become a golden copper palomino with a snow white mane and tail. Striking as he was, he had the cow sense and athleticism to back it up. He was a real contender for the Fort Worth futurity. (Back then the futurity was experiencing a growth spurt because of the excitement that Doc Bar horses were bringing to the arena. Doc Bar's get and grandget dominated the event for almost two decades.)

By November the futurity pre-works were in full swing in Lawton, Oklahoma, but Bill was still procrastinating as to which colt he would show at Fort Worth. Politics were involved — and probably cash — and at the last moment Bill decided to show another stallion. Doc's Summer Wages would be shown by me, a non-pro with no game plan.

In cutting you need two herd holders, who keep the herd centred, and two turn-back men, who prevent the cow you've cut from bolting. The turn-back men are extremely important, and I had no turn-back team ready for my first go-round. Thankfully Buster Welch showed up to fill the role and I rode into the herd. Yeller worked well, but I moved my rein hand just enough to get us eliminated; we did not advance. For us the big show was over. (Many years later, Bill Freeman would advise my friend Bill Riddle, "If you've got three good ones before the futurity, you're probably going to ride the wrong one." Hindsight is 20/20.)

After the Fort Worth futurity, I hoped Doc's Summer Wages would find success a year later at the Canadian futurity for four-year-olds. He did just that, winning both finals, open and non-pro. And he did it with a tendon that had been torn and healed — what horsemen call a bowed tendon. Doc's Summer Wages wasn't overly stud-like, but he was a charismatic horse with a flair for showmanship. In the arena, when I would bend over to put on his front splint boots, he would remove my hat with his teeth and wave it at the crowd.

One summer evening I was drinking a few beers with my friend Einar Brasso, a Calgary Nissan dealer who had an acreage at Priddis, just southwest of the city. We got to thinking what a great idea it would be to let Yeller breed one of his mares. What a grand gesture! Yeller was all for it, but when he mounted the mare, he fainted dead away in his freshman excitement. I thought he'd had a heart attack. "My God, we've killed him!" But presently Yeller recovered and finished the job.

Since Doc Bar and San Peppy bloodlines were very popular in the 1970s, I set about advertising Yeller as a breeding horse. We were able to attract some nice quarter-horse mares in Alberta and Montana, but few of outstanding quality. At the time I thought the Doc Bar blood could upgrade any mare, but really it's the mare who brings sixty percent of the quality — or lack of it — to the cross. As time went on, though, Doc's Summer Wages sired some nice colts, probably about a hundred in all.

As for Doc's Able Mable, she foaled her second Mr. San Peppy colt at the King Ranch in Texas in 1981. A blaze-faced

bay colt, Second Summer — I soon took to calling him
Bighead — could not have looked any more different from
his brother Yeller had he tried. That fall I picked him up at
the Giesbrecht farm outside Chilliwack, B.C., and was
amazed at his vitality. He'd hitched rides all the way from
south Texas to B.C. with Lord knows who, and the little guy
looked bright as a freshly minted loonie. The next morning
I hauled him home through the Rocky Mountains. Bighead
was a pleasure to start, a big, strong two-year-old with a
great attitude. I can't recall him ever bucking, and he loved
to work cattle.

Though these horse projects were still an extension of
my ego, I was continuously moving away from the "make
'em do it" mindset. Great cowhorses make themselves,
pretty much. If they have the bred-in athleticism and you
take the time to show them what you want — the very
basics, the straight stop, correct shoulder position and so on
— in time they'll put it all together.

After I moved to Pincher I was playing gigs on and off at
Ranchman's, the Calgary honky-tonk I'd been playing
when I decided to move to Alberta in the first place. I kept
taking week-long stints well into the 1980s. It was a steady
paycheque, about five thousand dollars a week. I had a pool
of local musicians on call and was usually able to cobble
together a band.

Ranchman's is a Calgary institution, the kind of place
where out-of-town journalists swing by to see what's happening — and not much is. It's a good place to get drunk
but it wasn't a good place to play creative music. Nobody

listened; it's widely known that music is the least of concerns for everybody at Ranchman's. The owner, Harris Dvorkin, is a good saloon operator, well set up for liquor sales, but when it comes to music, he doesn't get it. The only reason I kept playing there was because it was good money. If you weren't feeling negative going into that place as a musician, you damn sure started getting negative on the way out. It made me sympathize with musicians in the jazz era who had to contend with people clanging away in those supper clubs, ignoring the band.

I wasn't completely focused on music at Ranchman's, either. An incredibly attractive kid named Twylla worked there. When I met her in 1978, she caught my eye right away with her prairie charm and spectacular figure. She worked in the bar's self-serve, a glorified cafeteria that was a key part of the operation. The cowboys loved it because you could have your bacon-and-eggs breakfast there at two in the morning and sober up.

Twylla worked the self-serve by night and attended high school by day. At seventeen she could pass for twenty-one, and she had a maturity beyond her years. She had known tragedy and pain during a very troubled childhood in Rosebud, Alberta. Her dad hanged himself in the grain elevator he ran; afterwards, one of her brothers shot himself. The family moved to the city, but Twylla didn't get along with her mother at all. She ran away and was fast becoming a street kid when she found a refuge at Ranchman's, where Dvorkin took her in and hired her. Being a country kid, she worked hard.

All the guys at Ranchman's were after Twylla, but our physical attraction was immediate and mutual. I cut her out of the herd and ran her off. The Dvorkins were a lively bunch, with family members and friends coming and going at crazy hours. Half the time Dvorkin didn't know where anybody was, and Twylla would sneak off to see me whenever she could. When Dvorkin figured out what was going on, he was very upset about it; ever since, we've been at odds with each other off and on.

The south end of Calgary was abuzz with gossip about Twylla and me when we hooked up. At forty-four, people said, I was too old for her and she was too young for me. I didn't think that was the case then and I still haven't changed my mind. I wrote a song about it ("Nobody Thought It Would") for my 1994 album *Eighteen Inches of Rain*:

Nobody gave us a Chinaman's chance
Just a honkytonk romance, a tumbleweed dance
Who would have figured it would turn into love?

I was doing the classic Ian Tyson thing at this point: I really had no plan. What I did know is that I wanted to keep running with Twylla. She was both glamorous and capable. I thought the happiest years of both our lives lay ahead, and I was right.

CHAPTER 6

Sagebrush Renaissance

I wasn't following new music at all in the late 1970s. In fact, I only listened to two records while I was at Pincher Creek. The first one was by Mary McCaslin, one of the first contemporary western singer-songwriters. McCaslin was a California valley girl who fell in love with the desert and open range; she went on to give her take on the romance of the West in songs such as "Prairie in the Sky." Her records have a very appealing sound — usually just her voice and guitar, along with a bowed bass and a bit of French horn. The second record was by Al Stewart, the Scottish singer-songwriter who wrote "Year of the Cat." I have no idea why I had that record, but it grew on me after a while.

When Twylla came down to visit, all we'd listen to were those two LPs or the funky old Calgary radio station CFAC, which had a great Saturday night dance party complete with schottisches, reels and waltzes. As a result, I completely missed the British rock and roll era. Queen, AC/DC, Led Zeppelin — I missed them all. I didn't know about Crosby,

Stills, Nash and Young either. But while I was out in the sage-brush running steers with Alan Young and Uncle George, Neil Young decided to cut one of my old Ian & Sylvia tunes on his 1978 album *Comes a Time*.

The way Neil tells it, when he was a kid he'd go out to Falcon Lake in Manitoba and repeatedly listen to "Four Strong Winds" on the jukebox, putting in quarter after quarter after quarter. It came as a surprise to me when he decided to cut it. People think you're notified when somebody covers your song, but that's not true at all. They don't have to notify anybody. If the song is copyrighted under ASCAP, the royalties accrue over time and then a year and a half later you get a cheque. *Comes a Time* was a big album for Neil, and I got a handsome cheque in the mail. I was grateful because I didn't have much money at the time — I was scuffling.

The only reason I got that big cheque was because Albert Grossman's lawyer, David Braun, had taken good care of me when I was a naive folk star in the 1960s. Back when I wrote "Four Strong Winds" I didn't know a thing about music publishing and copyrights. Neither did Sylvia. Braun saved our bacon by putting clauses in our contracts that required the copyrights to revert from the publishing company back to me after a certain number of years. By the time Neil covered "Four Strong Winds" the copyright had reverted to me, which meant I got all the royalties instead of having to split them with the publishing company.

Truth be told, I thought Neil's version of the song was a little weird, and it took me a little while to get used to it. I thought the harmonies were strange, but I realized later that they were exactly right for that time. I was just too out of touch musically to see that at first.

I kept my music career alive by putting out a record of my own in 1978 — my first since 1973's *Ol' Eon*. Released on a funny little Toronto label called Boot Records, *One Jump Ahead of the Devil* was a mishmash of songs I'd recorded in Nashville, Toronto and Alberta. It wasn't bad at all though I was pretty half-hearted about music when the record came out. At least I was keeping the ball moving.

I was still at Pincher Creek in 1979 when I got the call from my realtor friend, Frank Watts, letting me know he'd sold my Ontario farm. (The neighbour with the landfill had finally decided to buy the place.) Between the land sale and my "Four Strong Winds" royalty cheque, I now had a fat chunk of money with which to buy some Alberta land where Twylla and I could settle down together.

John Scott, a friend of mine and a livestock supplier to the movie industry, told me about a bare quarter-section up for sale a few miles east of Longview, about an hour southwest of Calgary. It was right off the Cowboy Trail, a highway route that cuts through the heart of Alberta ranch country.

Enamoured with the possibility of having our own ranch, Twylla and I went to check it out. There was mud everywhere, but on the mud pan sat a beautiful log house. Behind it was a little coulee. To the east I saw miles and miles of flat buffalo range. To the west, a big front face of shining mountains, the same mountains that had wooed me to Alberta in the first place. The ranch itself was a little more prairie than I wanted — I preferred more foothills. But the foothills were close, and I really liked the idea of living in a log house. *This has potential for a horse ranch,* I thought, and I decided I wanted to live there. Twylla liked it too, although she said she didn't really care where she was, as long as she was with me.

We moved in during the winter of 1979 and promptly set about building the T–Y ("T bar Y") Ranch. Uncle George had registered the name with the provincial branding office while we were at Pincher. The T was for Tyson, the Y was for Young (Alan, not Neil) and the bar is where we all went to drink.

Twylla threw herself into the cowboy lifestyle and the building of the ranch, something that wasn't hard to do, since she was a country girl who wasn't scared of hard work. During the week she worked at an upscale western store in Calgary, and on weekends we'd pound fence posts and string barbed wire. It was a really happy time for both of us. To some degree I was probably a father figure to her, since she'd lost her real father — whom she was very fond of — to suicide as a kid.

Twylla's tough family situation even improved a bit once we moved to the ranch. We always had Christmases at our place and Twylla's mother and brother would come on over. Her mom would disagree with this and disagree with that, but at least Twylla had her family back. The ranch healed old wounds.

I especially loved when Twylla's grandmother Mrs. Hertz came to visit. In 1929 she had emigrated from Estonia to Oyen, Alberta, just west of the Alberta–Saskatchewan line — right in the middle of nowhere. That was back when the railroad lied to all those poor homesteaders to get them on the boats from Europe to the prairies. But Mrs. Hertz was a tough old gal, and she made the best of it, scratching out a new life and starting a family on the prairie. She was a good one. One time I roped a wild cow going across the backyard, and she thought it was the greatest thing in the world. "That's what they do here," she said ecstatically. "If the cow gets away, they rope it."

When we first arrived at the ranch, I was regarded as something of an outsider by the local community. It wasn't long before I fell in with a group of local cowboys: Bob Spaith, a sculptor; Steve Hoar, another sculptor; Rich Roenisch, yet another sculptor; and Gaile Gallup, who'd go to art school later and become a painter. It's not that unusual for a group of cowboys to be artists as well, although it's less common in Canada than it is in America. Some guys are rawhide braiders, some guys do horse dentistry, and a lot of them are artists.

It's hard to say how the cowboy–artist connection started. Maybe it goes back to the horse. Or maybe it goes back to Charlie Russell, who amazed all of us in the West with the genius and romance of his paintings. In any case, it's tradition now. Art is woven into the tapestry of the cowboy life. And it's not just a hobby, either. Cowboys need other arrows in their quiver because they can't make it on cowboy pay alone, and they often get screwed over by the ranches where they work. The owner will say, "You'll always have a home here, Bob," and then, six months later: "You've got two weeks to get the hell out of here." It happens all the time.

The local cowboys I met all worked at nearby ranches. I bred a lot of colts at the ranch back then, and each September

I'd have a really cool branding where we'd all get together and break out the Scotch and brand colts. Later, people got married and had kids, and eventually some got divorced, but at the time it was a cool, freewheeling group. We were the "wild bunch."

After we moved to the ranch, Clay came out a few times a year to visit. He and Twylla quickly became good friends (as Twylla rightly pointed out, she is much closer to him in age than she is to me). I'd also keep in touch with Clay by visiting him in Toronto when I went there to play the *Tommy Hunter Show* each year. Now a teenager, Clay had joined a boxing club in Toronto, which did wonders for his self-esteem. I never did see him box but I hear he was a pretty handy welterweight. His coach was an excellent influence on him.

The boxing phase was very good for Clay, but he still wasn't doing well in school. In high school he dropped out altogether. Looking back, I think his struggles were largely a result of Sylvia and me breaking up. Our divorce had been very hard on him, and after he dropped out he left home and became pretty angry — and I'm sure some of that anger was directed at me. He had issues with his mother too. Sylvia and I weren't talking much at this point but we were cordial, and I remember being surprised to hear her say that she didn't see him much more than I did — and they lived in the same city. When he cleared out, he really cleared out. That's the Celts for you.

After he left home, Clay studied music, learning to play the piano and bass. He tried to make it in the Toronto music scene but had a rough time with it. He would have had a better shot if he'd been there in the 1950s, like I was. It was a lot easier to get started back then; you didn't need as much talent and there were fewer musicians. By the time Clay was trying to make it, in the 1980s, the music scene in Toronto was very competitive, and having parents who were famous didn't help him any. It's a very common phenomenon in show business: the sons and daughters of famous people have a difficult time — they either try too hard or don't try hard enough. Clay was like his old man; he didn't know who he wanted to be.

He played bass for an alternative band called Look People in the late 1980s and early 1990s. They were absolutely crazy. Somebody described their sound as "demented jazz circus orchestra music." The drummer would play naked — except for his socks — on Queen Street West. Look People put out a few records, toured a lot and achieved a certain amount of notoriety, especially in Europe, but didn't have much financial success. When Look People toured in the West, they asked to stay in the little line shack behind my house. "You can all stay, but please don't burn the damn thing down," I pleaded.

As for me, I kept doing week-long stints at Ranchman's every month or two through the 1980s. I was a regular fixture there — me and Wayne Vold, a singer and bronc rider Twylla had been friends with since she started working there as a teenager. He and I quickly became friends too, and we eventually became neighbours when he put together his little outfit on Tongue Creek, north of our ranch, around 1990.

Harris Dvorkin had high hopes of turning Wayne and me into stars, but playing Ranchman's was still a drag. On winter nights I'd drive in from the ranch on icy roads in my dinky little Toyota and perform material I'd written, but I was just putting in time to pay for fence posts. Sometimes the crowd's indifference got to be too much and I'd snap at some loudmouth. I wasn't a young kid anymore but I'd get in a couple of licks — and then the bouncers would be right on me. At least I got the satisfaction of popping some guy a couple of times; it really helped alleviate my annoyance with the place. Honky-tonks like that can be fun for a couple of nights, but not six nights a week.

We did a lot of drinking those nights. I had the waitresses trained. When I was two-thirds of the way though the last set, they'd start bringing up the brandies and the cognacs. Then we'd pack it up and I'd drive home drunk. In all those years I never got busted. That wouldn't happen now since the cops have cracked down on that old saloon culture. If you get caught drinking and driving these days — especially coming out of a saloon — you're screwed. And I guess that's good.

Each July during the Calgary Stampede, Ranchman's became crowded, hot and sticky — full of girls chasing guys with gold buckles. I always looked forward to seeing one of our fans during Stampede week. Casey Tibbs — the most charismatic bronc rider of them all, a legend of rodeo — would tap on the back door of Ranchman's, I'd let him in and he'd sit in a dark corner and listen to us play. Calgary was a big town for Casey; he won the saddle bronc championship at the Stampede two years in a row, in 1949 and 1950.

Casey had a girl in every port, and when he came to Ranchman's he'd bring along his blond Alberta girlfriend. He had put on weight — no longer the slender young athlete who had won the world saddle bronc riding championship at nineteen. But he was a cool guy, and I knew old Casey would be there to see us every year. We always seemed to play better when he was around. I wrote a song for him before he died in 1990. *I'm the number one fan of the rainbow man,* I wrote, referring to his trademark colourful garb. *He's the wildest of 'em all.*

A mysterious Irish horse-shoer named Noel Hope also hung around Ranchman's. He was a fan of mine, and he'd often come out to the ranch to visit Twylla and me. One time he even flew out in a helicopter. He wanted to make a grand gesture, and it worked — he landed right in the corral. The ponies freaked, but Twylla thought it was great. She would cook us dinner and Noel would ask to hear the old Irish songs. Twylla also loved the old ballads and cowboy songs, and I'd play for them both.

Twylla was the one who got me into recording western music again. She believed in my songs when no one else did, and in 1983 I put out *Old Corrals and Sagebrush* for Columbia, singing about horses, ponderosa pines and the old Double Diamond Ranch in Wyoming. My friend Jay Dusard shot the cover photograph — a fine black and white picture of me sitting on Smoky, my circle horse, in front of the Diamond V weigh scales. *Old Corrals* was a cowboy record through and through, recorded in the basement of my ranch house. I dedicated the album to Alan Young.

When I first met Alan, he partied hard but also knew how to handle his life and work. He was likeable in so many ways and had plenty of loyal friends. But in the 1980s his life began to unravel. The drinking got heavier and heavier. Uncle George rodeoed and drank whiskey too, but he kept his eye on the ball the whole time. Alan just couldn't — the party always won out. It would cost him.

In the early 1980s Twylla and I made a habit of escaping the lousy Alberta winter by taking our vacation in January and February. We'd get some local guy to take care of the ranch — usually Twylla's brother Gord — pack up the truck, head south and find a little cowtown with a good bar and a restaurant. We'd hole up there for a day or two and then go on to the next cowtown and do the same thing. I didn't have to worry about playing gigs, and because there were no cellphones, my agent, Paul Mascioli, couldn't get hold of me. We'd just drive, totally carefree, all the way from Longview down to Prescott, Arizona, and on to Tucson.

Those winter getaways are some of the best memories of my life. We saw a lot of old friends and made a bunch of new ones, including Jay Dusard and another western photographer, Kurt Markus. We met them through the cowboy underground — Jay in Prescott and Kurt in Colorado Springs, where he was working for *Western Horseman* magazine.

Kurt had been an up-and-coming tennis player when he got whacked in the eye with a ball, which ruined that career. He wasn't a cowboy of any kind, but he had married one of Dick Spencer's daughters back when Dick owned *Western Horseman*. The magazine sent Kurt on an assignment to shoot some old cowboy in Nevada. He disappeared into the sagebrush of the ION — southern Idaho, eastern Oregon and northern Nevada — where he discovered a lost world of buckaroos, all-night saloons and whorehouses. That culture was still very much alive in northern Nevada, even in the 1980s. There was hardly any barbed wire north of Elko, all the way to the Idaho line. Kurt had found the Old West (just as Bing Crosby had a generation earlier when he bought the sprawling PX outfit, out on the Owyhee Desert, to contain his four Hollywood sons).

Environmentalists hadn't shut down the big cattle outfits yet, and operations such as the Allied Land and Cattle Co. could run cattle on federal rangeland in Nevada for a token fee. Herds of twelve thousand mother cows weren't unusual. Those operators would hire a tough cowboss and eight buckaroos, get ten horses for each kid, and send 'em out into the sagebrush with a chuckwagon cook to brand calves for three or four months. Every now and then the cowboys would head into town, buy a new hat, get drunk and go to the whorehouse. When Kurt found this lost world, it completely blew his mind. Being a really smart and inquisitive guy, he snapped pictures of everything, and in the process he became a brilliant photographer.

Kurt really showed me the ION, the buckaroo West. I'd fly into Boise, Idaho, where he would pick me up in his old brown Chevy van with his bedroll and saddle in the back. We'd head out to visit all the classic ranches — Maggie Creek in Nevada and Whitehorse in Oregon. Cowboys really liked Kurt because he'd stay out there with the buckaroos, freezing his ass off in some snowed-in cow camp when it was twenty below. They didn't know who the hell I was, but because I could ride and was with Kurt, they accepted me pretty quickly.

When we headed into the desert together, I was very careful to back-trail my landmarks. Out there you can get lost, really lost. Some of the kids I rode with told me they'd gotten lost and spent many hours finding their way back to camp. I didn't want to end up like that.

Half the time when Kurt and I were riding, I wouldn't even know he was shooting. That's what makes him great: the cowboys didn't know he was shooting either. He was like a quick-draw gunfighter. A bucking horse doesn't wait for a photographer to give it the cue, but Kurt could get the shot right away. He's the only guy who can do that, so he quickly made a name for himself in the West.

I was still working on making a name for Ian Tyson in the West. I went on tour with Ricky Skaggs — a fabulous picker — in both 1983 and 1984. The day before one of those tours, I broke my toe. My dog was messing with the cattle at the round pen; I went to kick at him and hit the gatepost instead. But on tour, my band and I more than held our own. One kind Ottawa reviewer even said we played better than Ricky. In 1984 I put out another record, titled *Ian Tyson*. (Stony Plain Records later merged *Old Corrals* and *Ian Tyson* into one album, *Old Corrals and Sagebrush & Other Cowboy Culture Classics*.)

Something strange happened in the 1980s. Cowboys became increasingly fashionable, thanks in part to John Travolta's *Urban Cowboy*, which came out at the beginning of the decade. But there was little reality in the urban cowboy trend. Those guys in the bars in Houston and Galveston weren't cowmen but day workers in the oil industry, working in processing and compressor plants during the day and putting on their cowboy hats at night before heading to the dancehall. It was all about dressing up. I think that's why I started emphasizing authenticity so much in my music. There were too many fakes around, too many people trying to convince the world they were cowboys.

It was the start of a weird dichotomy for me. I didn't like the phony cowboy movement at all, yet I directly benefited from it. Suddenly everybody everywhere wanted to know about buckaroos. When I went to Toronto with my band to play some club, young people came out in large numbers to hear us. Some of the girls were even wearing Dale Evans gingham. It was all pretty weird, considering I couldn't even get a job in Toronto a few years earlier. Now journalists were bugging me for interviews, wanting to talk about the West.

A cowboy renaissance was blooming in North America, and Elko, Nevada — one of the towns Twylla and I regularly hit on our winter road trips — would soon become ground zero for the movement. In 1980 it was a cowtown and railroad town with fewer than nine thousand people living there. There was a lot of Basque influence, from settlers who had come from the Pyrenees (between Spain and France) for the express purpose of herding sheep in the American West. I love that culture, and parts of it are still preserved in Elko. For example, Picon punch — a Basque drink made with a bitter orange liqueur — is the local drink of choice.

In January 1985 I travelled to Elko for a new event: the National Cowboy Poetry Gathering, organized by Utah folklorist Hal Cannon along with buckaroo poet Waddie Mitchell. Oral traditions were alive and well in that part of the world back then, since there was no TV and not much radio reception on those remote Nevada ranches. Hal, Waddie and a few other cowboys thought it would be great to get a few grants and celebrate those traditions by throwing a big party where cowboy poets could recite their verse. Hal had heard *Old Corrals* and invited me to come down and play.

The poetry gathering — or simply "Elko," as it came to be known — was also partly a reaction to the urban cowboy trend. "Though we didn't know it at the time, 1985 was ripe for ranching culture to reclaim its own story, to find the touchstones of its culture," Hal wrote in an essay many years later. "Cowboys had always allowed their story to be told publicly by others — songwriters, scriptwriters, novelists — but increasingly that story, told in popular culture, became a monolithic Arthurian myth, far from the breadth of the real life."

That first January, Hal and Waddie set up sixty chairs in the Elko Convention Center. Then they got nervous and put half of them back because they thought there weren't going to be enough people to fill them. Sure enough, their prediction had been way off — but not in the direction they expected. Somewhere between five hundred and a thousand people showed up for the damn thing. I just happened to be in the right place at the right time — again. My satchel was stuffed with western songs I'd written but hadn't yet found a market for. Elko changed everything for me.

Magic happens sometimes, and for me it happened that January. I had gone down with the perfect band. They looked great all dressed up. Neil Bentley, the chubby little bass player, wore a bowler hat; he played the role of storekeeper. Then there was drummer Thom Moon with his big handlebar moustache and black hat; he was the outlaw. Jeff Bradshaw, the pedal steel player, was the hillbilly. Myran

With Hal Cannon, co-founder of the National Cowboy Poetry Gathering in Elko, Nevada. (HEATHER HAFLEIGH)

Szott on fiddle was the dapper westerner who always wore a good hat and a sports jacket. And lead guitarist Gary Koliger was the wild Jewish guy from Edmonton. He didn't have a costume, but the buckaroos loved him anyway because he was crazy. All those guys could play. It was one of those bands that just have it.

Some of the folklorists got their noses out of joint when I showed up in Elko. They said, "Ian Tyson's a professional musician, hardly an authentic Nevada buckaroo." They didn't want me there and did their best to keep me out. There was a lot of controversy about it at the time, but Hal and Waddie stuck up for me, saying I was the real deal. We finally circumvented the whole controversy by playing Stockman's, a funky rundown casino, and blowing the roof off the place. Not only did people really listen to us, everyone loved us. The buckaroos and their girlfriends danced as if they couldn't get enough. Better still, none of them had heard of Ian & Sylvia, which was like getting a brand-new start.

The poets read what they had written at cow camps. None of them were musicians; you don't find many cowboys who play. You're either a cowboy or a musician, and there are very few who do both. Cowboys don't play instruments too well because their work is hard and their hands get all banged up. (There are some exceptions, of course, such as Mike Beck and me.) And then this Canadian cowboy shows up with five guys who can all play. That band's chemistry was serendipitous, and you couldn't stop it — it was like a tide. I must have had a hand in it, since I was the bandleader, but I know that the parts coming together like that was pure luck.

The next year we went back to Elko and played to even bigger crowds. The place was crawling with writers and media types representing everyone from the *New York Times* to *People* magazine. And it kept on growing every year. I realized, *Hey, I can make records of this music and there's going to be an audience.* I felt that there hadn't been a large audience for western music since the 1940s, when I saw Tex Ritter and the Sons of the Pioneers in Victoria. In my mind the only people who would pay attention to my music were a few cowboys in a bar in Elko, Nevada. But suddenly cowboy poetry gatherings were sprouting up all over the place. Some of them were just dumb low-budget events that were run so badly they died off, but others survived. I realized I could finally leave my Ranchman's days behind. The time was perfect for me and my songs.

Elko was the hub of the wheel, and the spokes went out in all directions. I started playing more gigs in California, New Mexico, Arizona, Colorado, Wyoming and Montana. Back at home, my band and I played the local bar in Longview and had people dancing in the street — literally. The cowboys and the girls from nearby Okotoks all came to see us. The crowd kept getting bigger and bigger, spilling out onto the deck and into the street. The cops came and shut it down while it was still light out, even though the whole thing was pretty mellow. I don't remember any fights. People dancing in the street is as good as it gets in Longview.

It would be a simpler story if I had gone to Elko, got excited about the possibilities of western music and returned home to write a bunch of songs. But that's not how it went down. My serious efforts in that regard actually preceded Elko; my satchel was full of western songs when I got there. It's really kind of spooky. It's almost as if I was being prepared to be the poet laureate of that sagebrush renaissance.

For most of my life I'd just drifted whichever way the wind blew. Now I had found my true voice in the West. I don't mean to trivialize Ian & Sylvia by saying that, but our duo was based on Sylvia's concept of harmony. Take that away and you'd be taking away the whole soul of the Ian & Sylvia sound. I hadn't found my own voice back in the folk days; it took years for my vocal style to evolve into something that was truly my own.

As a singer you start out trying to emulate your idols (the same is true of writers and other artists). I had several idols — Merle Haggard, Johnny Cash and Jack Greene, to name a few — and for a long time I was trying to sing like them. I was conscious of my vocal style, always trying to make it better, but I had to make my style my own. When a singer completes that evolution, the final voice is an amalgamation of a lot of influences, yet it somehow stops sounding like any of those influences and becomes itself. That's what happened to me in the 1980s. My style was almost there when I recorded *Old Corrals,* and by the time Elko rolled around, I really had it down.

Then I forgot about style altogether. I just opened my mouth and sang. I told stories. For better or worse, I didn't have to worry about finding an Ian Tyson style anymore. It was already there — I just had to use it.

As the West opened up to me, I wanted to learn more about it. A lot of people at Elko were writers, and the poetry gathering became a conduit for all this material I'd never encountered before. I'd return home from Elko with books by American writers including Larry McMurtry, Cormac McCarthy and J. Frank Dobie. (I don't think I read any Canadians back then. It wasn't a conscious decision — I just couldn't find anything that blew me away.)

Guys like McMurtry and McCarthy know how to write about the authentic West. McMurtry was ranch-raised and seems to come by it naturally in books such as *Lonesome Dove,* though I later learned that he based that story almost entirely on J. Evetts Haley's biography *Charles Goodnight: Cowman and Plainsman.* The writers I like are all research freaks. McCarthy isn't a cowboy and wouldn't pretend to be one, but he does his homework. If I had to write a book about a subject I knew nothing about — ore boats on the Great Lakes, for example — it would be a daunting task to do it credibly, since I don't know one end of a boat from the other. But McCarthy gets it right in books such as *Cities of the Plain.* I like his almost biblical narrative style, and he goes to great pains to describe the country and the flora and fauna, the flocks of birds flying at dawn. That really appeals to me; he's influenced me a lot.

I remember hearing an interview with Charles Frazier about his novel *Cold Mountain,* a beautiful piece of writing. I was deeply impressed by the authenticity of that book and wondered how he could portray the Civil War so realistically and credibly. In the interview he gave his answer: "Research, research, research." That was a big revelation to me. *I can do that,* I thought. I couldn't do it back in boarding school on Vancouver Island, because it would be about math or something I didn't care to know. But if it was about the West, I was more than eager to do the research.

I soon discovered fabulous bookstores in the U.S. such as Guidon Books in Scottsdale, Arizona. The store isn't that big but it's jammed from floor to ceiling with books on the West and the Civil War. That's all the owner, Aaron Cohen, carries. If he ain't got it, it ain't been written. Then there's the Tattered Cover in Denver, four storeys of great books. It's such a trip to go there. If the West is your mistress and lover, as Charlie Russell said, those are the places to be. I collected more and more books, building a western library. Today it's probably as good as any collection on the North American West. It's not massive, but every important book on the subject is in there.

Before Elko, most of my ideas about the West had come from my own experiences of it and from Will James — and obviously he wasn't a very reliable source. Now I was learning about the profound impact the horse had on Plains Indian culture, the glory years of the fur trade in the mountain West, and the monumental years of the cattle drives in the nineteenth century. That cattle-drive period, though brief — possibly only fifty years — had a tremendous impact on people's perceptions of the North American West. The cowboys herding cattle from Texas through Comanche country didn't know if they'd get to Colorado with their scalps intact. The drives spawned countless stories of western adventure, and as a result the cowboy and his horse captured the imagination of the world.

I became increasingly fascinated by the life and loyalty of the professional drifting cowboy. As a horseback labourer he had no social status at all, except with the whores in town and maybe the bartenders. But as Elko-born Bill Kane, former cowboss of the Spanish Ranch in Nevada, recalls, those drifting cowboys were incredibly accomplished at their trade. And they followed a completely different code from everybody else, creating their own culture with its own rules.

The cowboy was almost like a knight, bonded to the brand. Back in the Charlie Goodnight days, if Comanches attacked the trail herders a cowboy was fully expected to fight and to lay down his life if required. At the same time, if a ranch owner ever said something to ruffle the cowboy's pride, he'd say *adios*, roll up his bed and ride away. Being a maverick myself, the history of that free life on the open range appealed to me.

Devouring all this material on the West turned me into a western historian, giving me a third career in my fifties in addition to my horse and music work. I was definitely a late bloomer, but when the light bulb came on for me, it *really* came on — as I'd soon discover.

CHAPTER 7

Cowboyography

Right from the start, 1986 was a big year at the T–Y. At 6:30 a.m. on January 3, Twylla and I sped to the High River hospital full of excitement. After a tough delivery, Adelita Rose Tyson emerged to completely capture our hearts — a five-pound, one-ounce gift. From the get-go Twylla seemed happy just to have the baby at her side. Looking back, it's almost spooky how easygoing Adelita was, how she never cried at inappropriate times. She was an amazing baby, no trouble at all.

Within a week of her birth I was gone on tour, driving the truck and trailer south across the U.S. border. (Thankfully Twylla had support from her siblings.) The band and I were on the road almost constantly back then, building on our Elko success. Even before Adelita was born, Twylla had spent a lot of time holding down the ranch by herself — lonely nights with the chinook winds howling at the door and the coyotes crying on the hill.

On this particular occasion we were headed down to Salt

Lake City, with the drums hidden in the horse trailer. We had no visas, and because, as I mentioned earlier, border guys generally love to make life hard for musicians, we had to bluff our way across. The plan was to fly out of Salt Lake to New York City to play a party for Dan Lufkin, a New York investor I'd met at a Montana cutting contest the previous summer.

Lufkin is a real mover and shaker, but when I met him, I didn't know him from a hole in the ground. It was a hot Montana day and he was there with his girlfriend, Lindy Burch, and some fancy horses.

"Would you be the Ian of Ian & Sylvia?" he asked me.

Here we go again, I thought, and mentally rolled my eyes. "Yeah, I am."

"I used to listen to your stuff. I really liked it." He told me about a ranch he was building in Carmel, California. "Come on down sometime."

"Sure," I said, pretty sure he wasn't about to follow up.

He then told me about a big birthday bash he was throwing in New York in January. "Do you have a band?"

"Sure, I have a band," I said, though I didn't at the time.

"Would you come play for us?"

So that's where we were headed the week after Adelita was born. We parked the rig in Salt Lake, hopped a plane and played the NYC party. The society people didn't know what to make of us. I remember one woman saying, "That's the worst music I've ever heard in my life!" After all the society types went home, we played our hearts out for Dan and his architect buddy Jonathan Foote as they sat drinking hundred-year-old cognac.

That trip to New York for Dan's party was an important one for me because I met Tom Russell — another western singer and songwriter — for the first time the night after we played Dan's party. Tom and I had been corresponding since the late 1970s. One of my oldest fans, an English writer named Peter O'Brien, had given Tom my Pincher Creek mailing address, and Tom followed up by sending me a letter expressing admiration for Ian & Sylvia. He'd been a big fan during the duo's heyday in the 1960s. When we played L.A., he'd come to hear us at the Ash Grove, but I guess he was too shy to introduce himself. In his letter, Tom told me he'd written this song about a fighting cock, "Gallo de Cielo." Send over the tape, I told him, and he did. I loved the song and cut it for *Old Corrals*. We kept in touch afterwards but I'd never met him face-to-face.

I went to the rough part of Brooklyn where Tom lived — I remember being a little nervous about venturing into the area — and we hit it off right away. He was really unconventional, not just musically but also personally. His style was very western. He usually had a gun tucked inside his waistband. We're very similar, Tom and I. He's had a lot of women, maybe more than I have. And both of us are musical outsiders. Tom didn't fit into the New York scene but he struggled on, as I did. He was also a voracious reader, and his love for literature — Hemingway in particular — encouraged me to read more.

Soon after I got to Tom's place, we went and bought a couple bottles of Cabernet. "I've got a great idea for a song," he told me. "Here's the concept: two people in a café make love on a real nice old Navajo rug after hours."

"That's killer."

And off we went writing "Navajo Rug." We finished it over the phone — Tom in New York, me in a Fort Worth

Super 8 just off Interstate 30. I didn't know it then, but I had just started creating the pieces that would make up the biggest album of my career.

I kept writing songs all through 1986. At this point I hadn't yet bought the quarter-section with the little stone house, so my friend Einar Brasso kindly let me use his log cabin in the Alberta foothills for writing. After I got up in the morning, ate breakfast and fed the horses, I'd drive southwest for an hour to the cabin, which was just off Chimney Rock Road. It's pretty isolated. Once I got there I'd empty the mouse-traps and get down to work. The songs just came to me in that cabin nestled against the front face of the Rockies.

Late in the morning I would pack a sandwich, cross the creek and climb to the first plateau above the cabin. The climb was just hard enough. I'd see eagles and sometimes a black bear on my way up. And I never made that climb without getting something from it, even if it was only a line for a song. I'd stay there until 1 p.m. or so and then I'd come down, drive home and ride colts. When I came in at night, Twylla would have dinner waiting. She cooked a hell of a London broil.

Some of my best songs were written in Brasso's cabin, including "The Gift," inspired by an incredible painting Charlie Russell did during his last years. It was called *When the Land Belonged to God*. It's a huge canvas that hangs in the Montana state capitol building in Helena. When I first saw it, in typical Montana fashion it had been put in a dumb place with bad lighting (it's front and centre now), but despite the poor placement, it blew me away. It shows a herd of buffalo coming across the Missouri River, with a huge bull in the lead flanked by a couple of grey wolves. The water is pouring off the bull as he emerges from the bank, and you can see the whole herd behind him. The work is pure genius. The boys in the band used to kid me about it, because whenever we were driving through the area, I'd take a detour to see that painting and make them come and look at it with me. I just couldn't get over the thing.

In "The Gift," I imagine that Charlie takes over painting Montana sunsets from God. That was my little flash of genius, my tribute to the great Charlie Russell. For all of us in the West, he's our patron saint.

> God made Montana for the wild man
> For the Peigan and the Sioux and Crow
> But He saved his greatest gift for Charlie
> Said "Get her all down before she goes — Charlie
> You gotta get her all down, 'cause she's bound to go"

I figure that Russell had a gift from above. And when I was writing songs in Brasso's cabin for my new record, it was like I was getting a gift from above too. Those songs can't have been as easy to write as I remember them being, but I was definitely infused with a creative energy that came from somewhere outside of me. I just let it come inside and went with it.

One thing that didn't come so easily was finding a way to fund the record. I was determined not to use government funding. At the time, artists in Canada were getting their records subsidized with taxpayers' money, and I didn't think that was right. Gordon Lightfoot felt the same way.

We thought the subsidies were bullshit, and weren't afraid to say so publicly. We also didn't think the subsidy system would last long at all. In retrospect, though, I think I was wrong. The system seems to work, and these days all kinds of artists are making records with government money. But in my mind, if you want to make a record, you do it the old-fashioned way and pay for it without government hand-outs. Refusing government money is probably an obsolete stance, but I've been that way for a long time and can't see changing.

I finally solved the funding problem by getting two private investors. One was Einar Brasso. The other was Dan Lufkin, my New York friend, who likes to use his wealth creatively and constructively. (The ranch he'd invited me to in the Carmel Valley is a prime example, a fairytale place about twelve miles from the ocean, with rolling hills and moss hanging from oak trees. Twylla, Adelita and I used to visit and take along two or three horses to ride. Dan's ranch got all broken up after his divorce, but back then it was wonderful, a cowboy paradise.) Dan was very helpful when I approached him about investing in the new record. I don't know that he thought he'd get his money back, but both he and Brasso would end up getting a very good return on their investment.

The title for the new record was suggested by Neil MacGonigill, a Calgary promoter and manager who was a business partner at the time. He pointed me to a poem by Gail Gardner, one of the early cowboy poets, called "The Sierry Petes," which is a bastardization of "the Sierra peaks." It's a very famous old cowboy poem, and a very good one too. The lines have been altered here and there since Gardner wrote it in 1917, and in one version, a couple of cowboys are going to go get drunk on whiskey row when one of them says, "I'm tired of cowboy-ography, and I 'lows I'm goin' to town." There was my album title: *Cowboyography*.

I had all the ingredients for a magical record. Now I just needed someone to pull all the pieces together. That person was Adrian Chornowol, a brilliant but tragic character if ever there was one.

I had been working on a dinky but fun television show called *Sun Country* since 1982; it was one of the last half-hour country/western programs. Twice a month I'd drive up to CFRN in Edmonton to record the show. Adrian was the music producer. A piano player from a musical Ukrainian family, Adrian had worked as my vocal arranger on *Old Corrals*. He could play anything on the piano, from Rachmaninoff to country. As a musician, he was strong, focused and clear.

"I can produce a great record for you," Adrian told me. "The songs are absolutely terrific." Something inside my head said, *You know what? He probably can.* And so I took him on as my producer. We recorded *Cowboyography* at Sundae Sound in Calgary in August 1986. From the start it was obvious that Adrian had a vision for the record. He didn't know the front end of a horse from the back end, didn't know or care about cowboy culture, but he knew how these songs were supposed to sound. He knew that, musically, this could be a very strong record.

I remember him at Sundae Sound that summer, sitting amidst the rickety equipment. He'd be there working on some detail — the bass-line track, for example — for a whole night, recording on that analogue sixteen-track. He was basically living in the studio.

In the afternoon I would drive in from the ranch. I'd sing and Adrian would tell me, "That's a little out of tune there, Ian." Nobody had ever corrected me like that before. Where my previous producers would just let me screw up, Adrian wanted to get it right. He also knew how to arrange harmonies. Lots of guys say they can do that, but Adrian really could do it. He understood phrasing, and he wasn't shy about telling me how to phrase the songs. Most of the time he was right.

Looking back, I see a lot of naïveté in *Cowboyography*. There's a lot of romantic stuff in there I wouldn't write now — my outlook these days is much darker. But back then I was in a younger, romantic phase of my life. Twylla and I were very much in love, and I wrote about us in "Own Heart's Delight":

We make a good team, my lady and I
I couldn't ask for anything more
If you don't believe me
Just catch us tonight
We'll be the best dancers out on that floor

Twylla and I got married on September 26, 1986, after the *Cowboyography* recording sessions but before the album's release later that year. Our friends and family all came to St. Aidan's — a beautiful little Anglican church near the Bar U Ranch, south of Longview — and got stuck in the parking lot. It had rained for nine days and nine nights beforehand, and the ground was a quagmire.

We had a nice little country service, Twylla in her white wedding dress and me in my blazer, blue jeans and cowboy boots. My old troublemaker friend Bugsy Bigelow had shown up out of the blue a few days before the wedding, on his way to Montana. "You're going to be my best man," I told him — and he was.

At the wedding reception at the East Longview Hall that night, I danced with Twylla as she held baby Adelita in her arms. Almost eight months old, Adelita had her party dress on. I can still see her waving her arm like a tiny monarch as all three of us waltzed around the room.

Cowboyography was the Ian Tyson record with the magic. It came along at exactly the right time, and who the hell knows how that mystery works? Success happens or it doesn't — and most of the time it doesn't. All I know is that I couldn't have planned it better. *Cowboyography* coincided perfectly with the cowboy renaissance, and "Navajo Rug," "Fifty Years Ago," "Claude Dallas" and "Cowboy Pride" all got regular radio play.

Ironically, my business relationship with Columbia had petered out by this point. I didn't even have an American label when *Cowboyography* dropped in November 1986. I knew a big label would just screw it up anyway. The big labels don't know what to do with unconventional artists like me, and Columbia had more or less let my previous records languish, with minimal promotion. Instead of going that route again, I followed the lead of Baxter Black, an enterprising American cowboy poet who was merchandising all his books and cassettes himself and being very successful at it.

With Twylla and our daughter, Adelita. (JAY DUSARD)

With Roanie at the ranch. (JAY DUSARD)

Twylla and I put out *Cowboyography* on our own label, Eastern Slope Records. This was the golden age of mail order — well before Amazon and iTunes — and Twylla worked incredibly hard, stuffing records and cassettes into padded envelopes and sending them to stores all across the American West. In addition to running the mail-order business, Twylla also found some American distributor folks, such as Vickie Mullen in Washington, who helped get the records into the cowboys' hands. It was a very grassroots operation. At the same time, Edmonton-based Stony Plain Records released the album commercially in Canada (its distributor at the time was RCA Records). Holger Peterson, Stony Plain's owner, had been a fan of mine since back in the Ian & Sylvia days.

Our various distribution methods ensured that everybody in the North American West soon had an Ian Tyson cassette in his or her truck. The Canadian West may not be that big, but the American West is *very* big, and that's a lot of pickup trucks. In the U.S. my name spread by word of mouth through the cowboy underground, originating, of course, from Elko. My friend Blaine McIntyre, for example, spread *Cowboyography* around by hand. An itinerant saddle salesman based in Brighton, Colorado, old Blaino would always have extra cassettes in his truck. When he went on his travels, he'd sell them for me.

I think *Cowboyography* would have had a shot at winning a Grammy in 1987 had it been nominated. But we didn't have an American label lobbying on the record's behalf, which is the downside of the grassroots method. Eventually I got *Cowboyography* onto an American bluegrass label called Sugar Hill Records, but that turned out to be a big mistake.

They didn't understand the music and, like Columbia, they didn't know what to do with it, a fact they more or less admitted. In Canada, *Cowboyography* won me all the music awards, including the 1987 Juno for country male vocalist of the year. In the 1970s I had hated the idea of hanging in there with so little recognition, but now that doggedness had paid off. *Cowboyography* broke the log jam, and eventually it went platinum (more than a hundred thousand units sold).

You would think Adrian would be riding high at that point, having produced such a successful record. You'd think he'd have gotten all sorts of projects as a result. But he didn't — or he did and then screwed them up.

You couldn't invent a life more catastrophic than Adrian's. Back when we did *Sun Country,* the TV show, he seemed to have his shit together. And when we recorded *Cowboyography,* he totally had his shit together. He also produced my 1989 record, *I Outgrew the Wagon,* but after that the whole thing fell apart for him. I took him on tour; when we played New York, we had to watch him all the time or he'd disappear. He was hardly functioning because he was addicted to hard drugs. But we didn't find out until later just how crazy his situation was.

In 1989 Adrian got knifed in his Edmonton home by a Native kid and his sister; they really sliced him up badly. After he recovered, he considered getting a sex change — he said he wanted to be a woman — though he never went through with it. Needless to say, his sexual life was totally screwed up. He changed his name to Toby Dancer and drifted out to Toronto, where he led the gospel choir at Emmanuel Howard Park United Church. Tragically, in 2004 Adrian died of a drug overdose in Toronto. He was only fifty-one.

Without Adrian Chornowol, there wouldn't have been a *Cowboyography*. I'd have done a record but it wouldn't have been what it was. The sound of that album, the whole feel of it and all the production values — that was all Adrian. The vocal clarity was absolutely perfect. He had a vision, and why he had that vision is so mysterious, because he didn't show that command of the terrain at any other time or with any other project. It was as if a disaster named Adrian had been put on the face of the earth, and just one project suited him so well that he did an incredible job — and then went back to being a disaster.

After *Cowboyography* came out, I loaded up the twenty-four-foot aluminum gooseneck stock trailer with our equipment and headed out on the road with my band. When you get hot, you've got to take advantage of it or get out of the way. We did a lot of hard travelling and I loved being out there on the road. There aren't very many secondary highways in the West I haven't been down.

We really ripped it up in Medicine Hat, Alberta, at a place called the Westlander Inn. It was always party time at the Hat, and I think the people there considered me one of their own. The music was upstairs and the strippers were downstairs, all under one roof. Ronnie Hawkins, one of the original rockabilly guys, used to play there, and it would get really wild because he loved to party. He caused more trouble than I ever dreamed of.

In certain towns people just took to us, such as Billings, Montana; Bend, Oregon; and Sheridan and Jackson, Wyoming. I vividly remember playing the Wort Hotel in

Jackson. You could tell something was happening when the people there heard our music. It was as if they had been waiting for it for a long time but hadn't known what they were waiting for. When they heard us play, everybody smiled from ear to ear. The music clicked. In Bend I was almost like Elvis — the girls all crowded the stage and the organizers had to schedule another two shows in the high school auditorium to accommodate all our fans. The drama teacher was pissed about it, jealous that we were intruding on her territory, but we played anyway. Then we'd go a hundred miles down the highway and couldn't draw twenty people. We never could make it happen in places such as Casper, Wyoming. (Dick Cheney is from Casper, which pretty much tells you everything you need to know about that town.)

Not everyone who came to see us was impressed with what I was doing. We'd get into fights over "Claude Dallas," a song on *Cowboyography* about an Idaho buckaroo and trapper charged with killing two game wardens in Owyhee County in 1981. I wrote it with Tom Russell and we had got a bit carried away with the imagery, describing how the wardens were gunned down at Dallas's camp while trying to arrest him for trapping out of season. You could make a case that he had shot those wardens in self-defence or that he had murdered them. It wasn't clear at all, and that's what we said: *There's two sides to this story, there may be no right or wrong.* We didn't realize how sensitive the subject was. Dallas was in the news again because he'd escaped from prison in 1986. In those days you were either for the forest service or against it, and our take — *he may be the last outlaw* — was very controversial in the West.

The FBI caught Dallas in California in March 1987, a year after his escape. After he was released from prison in 2005, he phoned me once in the middle of the night. I was half asleep and I don't remember much of what he said. I think he was asking about the Chilcotin country in British Columbia, and I probably told him that it was gone — overrun with civil servants — that there was no frontier left there.

As we kept touring *Cowboyography*, I had an important epiphany. We were scheduled to play a rodeo dance in Kelowna, B.C., only it wasn't at the rodeo. It was at a big old roller rink on the strip north of town. *Oh shit,* I thought, *this is going to be another dumb gig,* and I bitched to Thom, my drummer, about how we never should have booked it. Back then, if I was in a bad mood I'd let it show on stage. One of the poets at the first Elko put it pretty well: "Ian Tyson's terrific, but he's so damn irascible." That poet had me figured out.

Well, that night at Kelowna, after all my complaining about how we shouldn't have come, the roller rink was packed. And not only was it packed, as the couples danced by the stage I could see them mouthing the lyrics to my songs. That was a big surprise — I'd never seen that before.

I had just enough brains to realize I had been given an incredible gift. *You can't be negative on stage like you used to be at Ranchman's,* I told myself. I'm not going to take the whole rap for being negative at Ranchman's — it was a damn negative place — but I decided there in Kelowna that, no matter what was going down in my life, I wasn't going to let it intrude on the shows. I resolved to be a professional. To this day I've stayed true to that. That choice has done wonders for my singing and my playing, and probably for my writing as well.

CHAPTER 8

The Changing West

My corner of the West has been good to me over the years. But it's a young man's country. I can't help but curse the Alberta weather when it's thirty below zero and I'm out trying to fix a gate hinge and can't feel my fingers. This land is a little too far north. The winters are hard on the livestock. I don't care what anybody says — when it's forty below and your horses and cattle are out in that cold, it's tough on them.

We're absolutely shaped by the weather, and you've got to be a survivor to make it through. In winter all we talk about around here is when we are going to get some spring. Chinooks bring days of relief with their warm winds from the west, but even chinooks are a mixed blessing. They melt everything, and then at night, when the temperature goes down a few degrees, it all freezes again. My yard becomes a skating rink. That's okay when you're nineteen, but when you're my age, you have to be careful. I only have to slip once to do some real damage.

The winter conditions here can turn on a dime, some-times with deadly results. In 1900, for example, two home-steading ranchers in this area — Jack Nichol and Gordon McConnell — left for High River with a wagon to fetch sup-plies. They set out in the middle of a chinook and were likely ill-equipped and unfamiliar with the country, so they didn't realize how fast the temperature could drop. A bliz-zard hit and they never made it back home, even though the trip was only about twenty miles. They froze to death at Stimson Creek, which is across the Highwood River just south of my place. It's a classic indication of the violence of our weather.

I've experienced some of that brutality first-hand. On the way back from Elko in the late 1980s (after selling some five hundred copies of *Cowboyography* at yet another sold-out show at Stockman's), I phoned Twylla as we passed through Dillon, Montana, to check in and see how she and little Adelita were doing.

"We're fine, but you'd better hurry home," Twylla said, "because there's a big Alberta clipper coming down from the north." At this point the storm was up around Red Deer or Edmonton.

"Okay, we'll hook it."

We kept driving and did fine until we got north of Great Falls, Montana, where we hit a big windstorm. Great, ghostly tumbleweeds came rolling straight at us down the inter-state, harbingers of things to come. I'll never forget those tumbleweeds bouncing off the truck. They came right out of the night — a very Gothic and surreal scene. *We're in trouble here,* I thought.

We gassed up at Conrad, just south of the Alberta border.

It felt like a chinook but you could tell the temperature was dropping fast. Sure enough, by the time we crossed the Medicine Line the temperature had plummeted. The border guy that night wasn't an asshole — he must have been an exception, because most of them are — and just waved us right through. "You guys better get going," he said, "because this is going to hit hard."

At Milk River — still 170 miles from my ranch — it hit. That blizzard was one scary son of a bitch. The snow flew horizontally and we couldn't see the road. Our windows iced up. Thom and I had to take turns walking on the shoulder of the road, shouting directions while the other guy drove, just so we could keep the truck out of the ditch. We were pulling a trailer with our equipment and the rest of the guys were behind us in the dually truck, which has four rear wheels. We were helpless out there in the twenty-below cold (about minus thirty Celsius). You can't survive in that kind of weather for very long. If you run out of gas or go off the road and aren't picked up right away, you'll be dead in hours. A lot of cattle died that night, both in rigs and on the range.

Finally we made it to the little town of Granum, where we checked into a motel. The next morning as we limped up the highway, we passed numerous cattle trucks jack-knifed in the ditch. We made it home safely, but the experience shows how dangerous the northern plains can be. We could have perished in that storm. If a truck had come along and run into us — which could easily have happened, because the other drivers couldn't see out their windows either — we'd have been knocked into the ditch and we'd have died. Ian Tyson and Thom Moon would have become a modern version of the two homesteaders who froze to death at Stimson Creek in 1900.

The climate hasn't changed much since I moved here — it's still violent as hell — but a lot of other things have changed. When Twylla and I moved here in 1979, our local village, Longview, was a sleepy little town with an elementary school and very few services. The bar was the social centre, of course. It was run by a bawdy old gal who always had boyfriends about twenty years younger than she was. An aged Chinese woman ran a convenience store, although that label was an oxymoron. It was in no way convenient. I don't think the proprietor had ever heard of best-before dates; you had to check those yourself.

An excellent mechanic from Saskatchewan ran the old-time stucco gas station on the corner; Bruce could fix any truck of any vintage. The highway that ran through town was unpaved back then, and south of town, more gravel roads led to the ranches. Logging trucks drove those roads but there was hardly any commercial traffic.

Today Longview has a paved highway but nowhere to get your truck fixed. We've got a liquor store, a post office and a wonderful steakhouse. And then there's the Navajo Mug, the coffeehouse I opened in a rickety old saddle shop in 2002 to give visiting fans an opportunity to buy Ian Tyson paraphernalia. (Pat and June, the ladies who run it, make delicious mince pies too.) But you can't even get a flat fixed in Longview anymore the way you could in the old days. You've got to go ten miles up the highway to Black Diamond.

The country around Longview has changed too. When I moved to the T–Y, the agricultural land in the area was all in quarter-sections — 160-acre parcels. Twylla and I used to ride our horses across the Highwood River to visit friends. But within a few short years, developers found ways to circumvent zoning bylaws and break many of the quarter-sections into smaller parcels, some even smaller than ten acres. And then the country really got fenced up. Now there are lots of five- or seven-acre properties, and around every one of those little parcels is a four-strand fence.

It's not just my part of the world that has altered like this. Such changes have spread throughout the West, and there's a simple explanation for it: people. It's a tired old refrain of mine that we never thought the West would fill up with people, but it did. And it took only twenty or thirty years. Open country is essential to the culture of the West, but a growing population means those wide-open spaces are doomed.

Back in the 1980s I could see that confrontations were on the horizon. I'm no genius and I'm not a tree hugger, but I could see that the destruction of the West was on the way. In southern Alberta that destruction announced itself in 1987, when the Canadian Forces revealed plans to buy the historic OH Ranch near my place and turn it into a military training ground. A lot of guys around here thought that if they pretended the threat wasn't there, maybe it would go away. But it wasn't going to go away, and I knew it.

The OH is one of the oldest ranches in this area, home to all kinds of wildlife: wolves, cougars, bears, elk, eagles, owls and so on, as well as native fescue grass. That fescue rangeland is vital for wildlife, livestock and the entire prairie ecosystem (fescue roots grow up to three metres deep, storing carbon and water underground). Once that native grass is ruined, it's very hard to restore — the thistles and weeds take over. Regardless, the army was poised to push all the wildlife out of that country and rip up the land. You couldn't come up with a more inappropriate or ignorant plan if you tried.

There are certain people in the world who like to find a little paradise like the OH and completely change it. I don't know why that is, but it's a sad reality. In the case of the OH, the owners were having financial trouble — ranchers always are — and they saw the government's offer as a solution. I decided to step in, along with Tommy Bews, a well-known cowboy in the Highwood Valley, and his brother, Joey. Their ranches bordered the OH, so their involvement was based on self-interest (but what isn't?). We were up for a fight, and we went at it.

Tommy and I did our best to get the situation into the papers and on TV. I had a conduit to the media because *Cowboyography* was hot, and Tommy, a Canadian rodeo legend, was a real hero in those days too. We made a pretty good combination, and we stood off the Department of National Defence until a local oilman, the late Doc Seaman, stood up and bought the OH. There's a definite irony there, because Doc was an oil and gas man if ever there was one. But some of those guys love ranching and the cowboy life-style too. That's how the OH got saved. Now the provincial government has protected parts of the ranch as a conserva-tion areas, allowing for traditional ranching methods to carry on there.

It's good for cattle country when extremely wealthy people want to be cowboys. In fact, it's the best thing that could happen. It's been proven time and time again that deeded land in the West is always stewarded better than public land. People such as Ted Turner and Ralph Lauren may have an excessively romanticized vision of the West, but by controlling huge blocks of good rangeland they're helping the environment. Those rich guys may not be environmentalists, but the environment still wins. We need more guys like that here in Alberta.

The traditional ways of herding are good for the land. In purely ecological terms, the old style of open-range ranching — in which the cowboy moved with the cattle across vast territory — was exactly what nature wanted, because it mimicked the buffalo migrations. The cattle grazed and moved on, and the buckaroos were migratory herdsmen just like Mongolian nomads. Those old-time buckaroos were, perhaps without knowing it, friends of the grass, friends of the ecosystem.

Truth be told, there's no way that free-range era of moving with the cattle could have lasted for any length of time. In the early 1900s, big American outfits such as the Matador and the XIT briefly leased huge chunks of prairie range from the Canadian government for cheap. But then Ottawa decided the government didn't have enough control over that arrangement. It was too unruly and fast-moving and free ranging, and they were paranoid about American cowboys packing guns in Canada.

Ottawa didn't want wild young troublemaking guys coming across the border and bringing lawlessness to this country. Instead they wanted to open it up for the homesteaders, give them their 160-acre parcels and make those poor sons of bitches pay taxes before they started eating gophers and starved to death — or ended up broken in the flophouses of the West Coast. That's how it went down; the Canadian government has never regarded cowmen with much respect.

So we won a big victory when we saved the OH from the government's absurd plans. But that was immediately followed by another fight. The Mormons in the Cardston area of southern Alberta wanted irrigation water, so the Alberta government planned to build a dam on the Oldman River to give it to them — another terrible idea. When you dam something up, especially on the prairie, it fills with sediment. A steady flow of sediment nurtures the riparian areas alongside the rivers and creeks, and that's how cottonwoods grow. Take away the flow of sediment and you aren't going to have any cottonwoods. But those Mormons wanted irrigation water, period. I started working with Cliff Wallis of the Alberta Wilderness Association, a group that was leading the fight against the government's dam plans. Again I figured that my role was to bring attention to the situation.

My old friend Alan Young respected my stance on the Oldman Dam but didn't understand what was at stake. He had no problem with the extractive industries ripping up the West. Back when we were at Pincher in the late 1970s, Shell had built a big plant nearby and the company was laying pipelines all over the place. "Don't let them do that," I'd tell Alan, and he'd just roll another cigarette. It never occurred to him to put up a fight. I had always looked up to Alan, but his indifference saddened me. He could have been a positive role model, a force for good, but he just wouldn't take that step.

By the time the Oldman Dam fight rolled around, Alan had been ravaged by cigarettes and whiskey. After years of living the quintessential western life, he died in an old-time cowboy way, drinking himself to death like Will James. Alan died in a Calgary hospital the night of March 13, 1989. Days later, I sang "Amazing Grace" at his funeral in Pincher Creek. I still think about Alan a lot. He was a good friend, always fun to be around and always there for me, as much as he could be.

As the fight over the Oldman Dam heated up in 1989, I came up with an idea: we could throw a hell of a concert right by the river at Maycroft Crossing, make it free and ask for donations for the cause. To this end I brought in Gordon Lightfoot, Murray McLauchlan and Sylvia, among others. Somebody donated a sound system and power generators and we set up on a couple of big old flatbed trucks. People in the music community will usually give to a good cause, but often you've got to prod them, give them a plan and a vision. So that's what I did.

We got lucky with the weather on June 12, 1989 — it was perfect. Thousands of people came out, tree huggers and cowboys alike, and camped out at the crossing for the day. The buckaroos from the Waldron camp, a few miles away, loped over on their horses and rode around looking colourful. The local Peigan Natives, who opposed the dam project too, set up their tepees. Gordon performed his "Canadian Railroad Trilogy," Murray sang "The Farmer's Song" and Sylvia and I did a few songs together too — one of those impromptu Ian & Sylvia reunions. During the concert we passed around the hat, and we pulled in around twenty thousand dollars for the fight.

We did come pretty close to stopping the dam. The fight went all the way to the Supreme Court — which ruled that an environmental assessment for the project was necessary — but those Mormons were bound and determined to get their water. In the end they prevailed, despite all the good arguments and evidence against it. Even though we lost, the attention we brought to the dam forced the government to take more seriously the needs of fish and trees — and to change the way it operated the dams in light of those needs. That's been good news for the cottonwoods downstream.

After the Oldman loss I started becoming more cynical about this country. I'm talking about the way it operates, not the rocks and the trees. I had never been a political guy before and I'm a little sensitive about politics, probably because Sylvia and I always got a bad rap in the folk days because we were more into music than protest. But when it came to my beloved open West, getting involved in political causes just felt natural.

Ever since the late 1980s I've taken on the role of celebrity spokesperson for ranchers in this area. In 2006, Compton Petroleum Corporation of Calgary wanted to drill exploratory wells in the eastern slopes of the Rockies west of my place. The locals wanted me to get the situation into the media, so I took up the cause and headed into Calgary with John Cross of the a7 Ranche (he's the grandson of Alberta ranching pioneer and Calgary Stampede co-founder A. E. Cross) and Pokey, my mare.

I was supposed to ride Pokey at the McDougall Centre, the provincial government's headquarters in downtown Calgary. I was apprehensive because I thought she would spook on the pavement and tear my knee up, and then run over a bunch of people. Pokey's like that — she'll buck you off at the drop of a hat. But my worries were unfounded. She thought the whole thing was great. She loved all the noise and the clatter and the big tall buildings. We rode right up the building's front stairs. Bud, my gelding, would not have tolerated it, but Pokey absolutely loved it.

It turned out that the event didn't have media legs. It didn't matter, though, because Pokey made the experience a lot of fun. Hell, she wanted to go out for lunch and drink martinis afterwards. It was another reminder that horses are nothing if not mysterious. You never know what's going on in their heads.

These days I'm still helping out local ranchers and conservationists who are trying to preserve the eastern slopes for future generations. Suncor, a Calgary oil and gas company, wants to drill sour gas wells and build a big pipeline out on the slopes that would cut through pristine land. The damage would be incalculable. All these oil and gas projects require new roads, and it's the roads that really screw everything up. They get built along the line of least resistance — in other words, in the wildlife and water corridors. I'd been hoping the government would have the sense to not approve the Suncor project, but then it went and did it — business as usual in Alberta.

I try not to get too preachy about all this. You can't blame the people working in the industry for these problems — they're just trying to make a buck. But if you rip up the eastern slopes of the Rockies for short-term profit, what have you got then? That's the heritage of Alberta.

—

It's not just the landscape that's changing. The entire field of agriculture has undergone radical changes in the past couple of decades. I didn't know anything about large-scale agriculture when I started ranching, probably because there wasn't much of it around here then. But then the agricultural industry exploded. Companies figured out ways to house chickens in huge numbers — in the most inhumane way — and then how to do it with hogs, in equally inhumane ways. Now there are feedlots for cows and even horses. But nobody thought about what to do with all that manure. No one considered the runoff into the rivers and riparian areas, and what effect that would have on the ecosystem.

We North Americans want an endless supply of cheap food, and we want it retailed to us in the most convenient manner so that everything is just as simple as can be. But that simplicity comes at a big cost, and now it's all coming back to bite us on the ass. We've got all kinds of environmental problems and we're injecting hormones and steroids into these animals — all for corporate moneymaking. Consumers, meanwhile, are completely removed from the realities of what's going on. They don't see the poor chickens or hogs in those inhumane conditions. Out of sight, out of mind.

Ranching as I learned it was much more holistic — and still is. In the cow–calf business, cattle have a couple of really nice years before they walk that last mile. Even cattle in feedlots live in way more humane conditions than fowl and hogs.

If I were starting over again, I would put more time into working for the humane treatment of domestic animals. The way we treat them diminishes us as human beings capable of creative thought and compassion. Adelita used to comment on that when she was a little girl. "It's terrible the way they treat those animals," she'd say. (I've always hoped that Adelita will find a career working for the welfare of animals, maybe as a lawyer. She's certainly bright enough to do it, and is now working on a master's degree at a college in Texas.)

There's a push now to eliminate cattle branding as inhumane, but that's nonsense. The brand is momentarily painful but those calves are pretty tough — an hour or two later they're sucking on their moms' udders and they're okay. Branding is nothing compared to the terrible existence of industrially raised chickens and hogs, but that industrial system is dug in pretty deep now, and the farmers and ranchers find themselves stuck in a bad situation. It's the corporations that are crunching the numbers and setting the methods.

If I can find free-range chicken breasts at the grocery store, I'll pay the extra money. And if enough consumers decide they don't want to buy chicken that has been raised inhumanely, the system will change. It's as simple as that. You can see it already with companies such as McDonald's that are slowly changing their practices.

We need a major agricultural revolution. I'm fascinated by the grass-finished beef movement, in which ranchers raise livestock on marginal grasslands — terrain that's not prime agricultural land. Canada's got lots of that marginal land; Ontario, for example, is full of it. The area where I used to farm there is short on quality topsoil, it's very rocky and it's thinly covered. Cows can be finished on that grass instead of being stuffed with barley in a feedlot — it just takes longer. (In the old cowboy days it was common to raise steers for three years, but today most North American hamburger comes from sixteen-month-old steers. That's as far as they get before they're slaughtered.)

People in Morocco have the right idea. I visited the country in early 2010, and I could see that, unlike North Americans, Moroccans utilize *all* their land. Sheep and goats are everywhere. If Canada followed Morocco's lead, all our grassy ditches would be full of animals (and in Morocco I never once saw a sheep or goat step into traffic). That land would be more productive.

Ironically, it's the city dwellers who seem to be catching on to the need for an agricultural revolution. In Detroit, for example, people are turning vacant land into urban gardens. There's also a big movement supporting people in cities who want to keep chickens in their backyard for the eggs. And why the hell shouldn't they? I think it's great. Have a goat back there too, for milking. That's why I love Tucson, Arizona. The Mexican-Americans there all keep chickens in their yards, and the first thing I hear in the morning from my downtown hotel room is cocks crowing. I can't think of a better way to wake up.

While urbanites are learning to raise chickens in their backyards, ranchers are driving cattle with ATVs and training horses in big indoor arenas. That was never my idea. I always wanted to be out on the hills, in the mountains, on horseback. But there are very few real cowboys left. New Mexico still has a few because they can't grow wheat or anything else down there; the land won't permit it. My friends John and Jean Brittenham run cattle on many sections of New Mexican mesas and canyons and don't even own a tractor or a baler. John does, however, use a rickety grader to keep the red clay roads open when it rains. Other than that, it's a horseback deal.

That's what I love about New Mexico: nature has made sure that all you can do is run livestock — sheep, goats and cattle. And the terrain is such that you can't herd the animals with ATVs. You've got to do it either on horseback or on foot. You might be uncomfortable but at least you're outside, which sure as hell beats being stuck in some dark arena.

Being outside is a romantic element of the cowboy life, just like the six-gun. You can't divorce romance from reality in the West, because the whole deal has been romantic right from the beginning, all the way from Manifest Destiny onwards. The romance stretches from gunslingers such as Pat Garrett and Jesse James right up to today.

I was lured to the West by Will James, by Native cowboys in purple satin shirts, by the paintings of Charlie Russell and the cowboy photographs of Jay Dusard, Bank Langmore and William Allard. Allard's photos of people in the West startled me when I first saw them. Although they were taken in the 1960s, they looked like they were from the 1880s. I thought, *Who are these people?* I had to find out. And a bunch of other people — photographers, songwriters, painters and so on — had to find out too.

You can't separate romance from the West in the same way that you can't separate Hollywood from the West. They constantly feed off each other. Hollywood reinvented the West and kept on reinventing it, and then the characters of the West started imitating Hollywood cowboys. It's life imitating art. That's what the folklorists didn't understand when they tried to keep me out of Elko in 1985. They didn't want me around because, in their minds, there was a true West and a fake Hollywood West, and they thought I was part of the fabrication. But there is no pure West. You can't make a credible case for that separation.

In my part of Alberta, for example, the movie industry is huge. A lot of westerns have been filmed in the Longview area, including Clint Eastwood's *Unforgiven*. Hollywood is a big part of Longview's economic existence. There are operations out here, such as John Scott's ranch, where the cowboys and the longhorns are maintained just for the movies. If it wasn't for the movies, they wouldn't be working. And when the movie people come to town, they buy their gasoline at the local Fas Gas, their steak at the Longview Steakhouse and their coffee at the Navajo Mug. Hollywood stimulates the local economy in a very direct way. It's all part of that leisure industry that my dad couldn't get his head around.

I remember when you couldn't easily buy a pair of Levis or a cowboy hat or boots. That's how it was when I was a kid in B.C., and that meant there was no easy access for the wannabes of the world. I remember buying my first snap-button cowboy shirt — in Seattle, strangely enough. It cost seven dollars, a lot of money at the time. The shirt was green and I hated that colour, but I was going to buy that sucker because it had the snap buttons.

Now there's a massive western apparel industry for people who want to play cowboy. The reality is that, economically, the West needs that wannabe element. If you allowed only the remaining cowmen to be part of the West — the hardscrabble on-the-land ranchers raising their

Near the Oldman River in Alberta, in 1999. (© TODD KOROL)

cattle — there wouldn't be much here. I certainly need that element. My concerts absolutely won't happen if I don't have the wannabes. I love it when the authentic guys come, but there aren't so many of them anymore. My songs allow people from all walks of life to enjoy the West vicariously.

With *Cowboyography* I became one of those people who portray the romance of the West. Some would say I also became part of the problem. Someone once told Kurt Markus and me, "The West is fucked now, and it's your guys' fault. You put the final nails in the coffin." They meant that we had blown the cover of the hidden West of the buckaroo and inspired all these idiots to move in on the terrain. But that view is kind of selfish. Everybody wants to be the last one in, the last person to discover the West before it disappears.

CHAPTER 9

Beef, Beans and Bullshit

I've always liked Scotch, but in 1990 my days of drinking it appeared to be over. I got very sick while touring the Maritimes, and by the time I got back home from the tour, the illness had developed into pneumonia. Soon I could hardly function.

"You're going to the hospital," Twylla told me.

I didn't know what the hell was wrong with me, so I followed Twylla's advice and went to the High River hospital, checking into Emergency. Turns out I had a group A streptococcus infection. It scared the hell out of my doctor, Keith Spackman, because that same virus had killed Muppets creator Jim Henson the previous week. (Jim had got pneumonia and died in a matter of days.)

I was pretty out of it, and Dr. Spackman was terrified. "I just treated you like a steer," he joked later. "I ran you into the chute and didn't know what medication to give you, so I IV'd you and gave you everything."

It was a close call. I don't remember anything about

Riding Bighead (Second Summer) at the Tropicana Futurity in Las Vegas in 1988. (COURTESY IAN TYSON)

those days when I was hooked up to the IV. Whatever Keith did obviously worked, because I slowly recovered. But I'd developed asthma from the experience, so Keith sent me to see a diagnostician up in Calgary.

"It'll probably go away," the diagnostician said of the asthma.

Wonderful, I thought.

But he had a few questions for me. "What do you drink? Scotch?"

"Yeah."

"No more."

Shit.

"Wine?"

"Yeah, some."

"Red or white?"

"Red."

"No more. The tannic acid is bad for you. Vodka's probably your best bet — or a nice Chardonnay."

The rest is history. My asthma lasted for four or five years and then it was gone. White wine became my drink of choice because it's easier on the body. All my buddies thought I was nuts back then, but they're all drinking Chardonnay now too.

After I got out of the hospital in High River, I set about starting a beautiful filly given to me by Dan Lufkin. She was an own daughter of Doc O'Lena, one of Doc Bar's most famous sons, and we called her Roanie.

I used to be able to swing the saddle onto Roanie with one hand. Now I could barely lift it. *If Roanie breaks in half,* I thought, *I'm in trouble.* Somehow she didn't, which is very strange, because Roanie always seemed to do the wrong thing. Later that year she bucked off the woman I'd hired to work for me — twice. But she never did buck with me. Maybe she was taking pity on me in my weakness.

Not all our horses were that kind, however. Old Pin Ears jumps to mind. Of the many colts raised on the Tyson ranch in the 1980s and 1990s, Pin Ears was one of the most colourful. Dan Lufkin, breeder of the great horse Missin' Cash, had given me a breeding to one of his young studs around 1989, and the result was a bay colt foaled at my ranch, outside on a raw, wet March morning. The colt was okay and nursing well but I could see that the tips of his ears had frozen. Other than that, Pin Ears was fine.

I started him at age two when he was a green colt — a little on the slow side. He'd buck a little but it was nothing to lose any sleep over.

Then, in his third year, on July 9, 1992, Twylla was riding Pin Ears in the round pen when he started bucking. She flew off, landing stiffly in a manure pile. It happened in an instant and there was nothing we could do to change it. The fall broke her back. We were all traumatized by the accident. Adelita was six at the time, and we didn't know if her mom would ever walk again. But Twylla's surgeon did a miraculous job of putting pins into her back. In a matter of weeks she was up and walking (thank God for Canadian health care).

Twylla didn't ride much after her accident. Over the years I've been bucked off horses many times, and although I've broken my wrist, ankle and ribs, I've never been that seriously hurt — I know how to fall. But in September 2009, one of my colts got mad and came apart on me in the round pen. On the fourth stiff-legged jump, I knew I was in trouble. I took a big spill and my boot hung up when I came off. Thankfully I shook it loose. I was okay, but that scared me. It's the first time I remember being seriously scared about riding. I've been bucked off lots of ranker horses, but this was different somehow. It finally made me understand why Twylla had stopped riding after her back injury.

Everybody involved with horses gets injured eventually. It's the law of averages. You can't spend your life with them and not get hurt, even if it's just from the wear and tear on your body. I had my left knee replaced not long after Twylla got hurt.

Years later I got pretty beat up at the same spot where Twylla had her accident, thanks to a buffalo I kept at my ranch. I had about eight of them at the time for training cutting horses. Buffalo are great for training because when you put them in a round pen, they move in a predictable pattern. Unlike a cow's turns, a buffalo's turns are pretty much in the same place every time. That repetition and predictability help a horse learn how to cut.

Buffalo enjoy doing bluff charges: they'll run twenty feet towards you and then stop. But as far as my cutting horse Bud is concerned, there's nothing fake about a bluff charge. To him it's the real thing, and one of the buffalo came at him while I was riding in March 2004. Bud panicked and, because he wasn't shod, when he spun around, he slipped on some ice and went down with a bang. When he scrambled back up, I was hung up in the stirrup.

Here we go, I thought. Sure enough, Bud started dragging me across the prairie. I was using heavy brass oxbow stirrups, one of which flew up and whacked me in the face, swelling my eye closed and gashing my forehead. (Cowboys love the narrow, rounded oxbow stirrups because they have a good feel, but they're dangerous because you can't get your foot out easily.)

I finally came loose when my boot came off. I asked myself the usual question: *Am I alive?* Quickly followed by *What's broken and what's not?* I staggered back to the house, took a big double shot of vodka and said to myself, "Well, you've survived another one!"

For the next few days I looked like I'd been through five rounds with Evander Holyfield. The tissue around my replacement metal knee was all beat up too. I called my sister

Jean in Victoria and asked if she had any plans for the next couple of weeks. No, she said. Within days we were on a plane to Barcelona, Spain, where I hobbled around on crutches, visiting the museums and tapas bars until I could walk crutch-free again.

With horses you have to make a decision: is it worth getting hurt or not? I certainly believe it's been worth it.

After Twylla's accident in 1992, a Montana saddle-maker friend of mine, Chas Weldon, invited me to a calf branding to be held at cowboy poet Wally McRae's ranch at Forsyth, Montana. This convivial May affair, aptly named "Beef, Beans and Bullshit," brought together about a dozen artists in the western disciplines — saddle makers, rawhide braiders, painters, assorted shady characters — for three days of riding, roping and raconteuring. Everyone brought along his own horses. The gathering quickly became an annual tradition, something we all looked forward to every year.

Because of Twylla's injury, I wanted to find Pin Ears a new home, and what better opportunity than Beef, Beans and Bullshit? I had Wally McRae in mind as a potential buyer. But, having had a Scots mother, I should have known that McRae would be as Scottish as his name and that selling Pin Ears to him would be tough.

Pin Ears killed the sale for good by blowing his cork as we trotted up the ridge the next morning to begin the gathering. If ever there was a time for an Ian Tyson bronc ride, this was it. Horse sale or no horse sale, I didn't want to get bucked off in front of these guys. So I stuck my feet up front and made a ride, spurring the shit out of Pin Ears. All the

At the Beef, Beans and Bullshit gathering at the OW Ranch in Montana. I'm the one holding the branding iron. (COURTESY IAN TYSON)

Giving a concert before supper at Beef, Beans and Bullshit.
(COURTESY IAN TYSON)

guys — Chas, Joe Beeler, Les Best, Bill Reynolds, T.D. Kelsey, Hank Esp, Bob Douglas and Don Butler — looked on, oohing and aahing as Pin Ears farted around in a circle. I got him rode, and I was feeling jazzed about it.

But Wally said, "You're not injecting that bronc into me, laddie!"

The next day I quietly approached Bob, a horse trader. "I don't want to take this horse home and Wally's not going to buy him. Can you use him?"

"I think I can get three thousand dollars for him. Sure, I'll take him."

So Pin Ears left Twylla's and my life and we were three thousand dollars richer. That was the end of that — or so I thought.

Years later I was checking out boots at the Paul Bond Boot Company shop down in Nogales, on the Mexico–Arizona border. That's an important place in the West; Paul Bond is *the* iconic boot maker for working cowboys, and his shop is a depot for the cowboy underground. As I browsed I heard someone calling my name in a southern drawl.

"Mister Tahson! Mister Tahson!"

I turned around and saw two cowboys.

"My name's Rusty," one of them said, "and this here is Spider. When I's at the Matador in Montana, I had a horse in my string with your brand on his left hip."

"You've got to be kidding! Did he have frostbit ears?"

"Yessir."

"By God, that's ol' Pin Ears! Did he buck any guys off?"

"Yessir."

I couldn't believe it. Bob had sent Pin Ears out to the big outfits, and that troublemaking little bastard had become a legend, trotting across the whole expanse of the West as if he came right out of a Mike Beck song.

Beef, Beans and Bullshit was always a lot of fun. We'd go to a different piece of cattle country every year and we'd have a good chuckwagon cook who used a Dutch oven to prepare the beef and beans over the fire. It was a classic tree-house deal — no girls allowed — so the cook was always a male. The other guys drank whiskey and beer and ribbed me for drinking my Chardonnay. And every night I'd give the boys a concert. They were a wonderful audience. If a couple of guys wanted to talk, they'd go do it someplace else.

One year we had the gathering at a ranch about three miles from Bannack, Montana, the capital of Montana Territory in the 1860s. That's the best ghost town I've ever seen. We rode over through the sagebrush — it grows chest-high in that area — to investigate the old buildings. Bannack is in high-altitude country, cold and dry, which explains how the buildings have kept their integrity after all these years. The hotel is still there and the jail even has the leg irons in the floor.

In later years we met up at the OW Ranch in southeast-ern Montana — another historic place, birthplace of the Kendrick Cattle Company. The owner, Jim Guercio, had lovingly restored the buildings of the headquarters, and we stayed in the beautiful old bunkhouse, which looked as if it had come right out of a classic western film. The barn had enormous old cottonwood beams that were quite low, and Bob told the story of a buckaroo who came to work for the ranch and bought a new saddle. He cinched it to one of the broncs in the barn, and immediately the horse came apart, bucking into the beam overhead and smashing the saddle tree (its wooden framework) all to hell. Apparently the cowboy sent for another saddle, and the exact same thing happened again.

At the end of every Beef, Beans and Bullshit, Joe Beeler would make a pen-and-ink sketch of a face or a bronc and we'd all sign it. Those drawings were highly prized, as Joe had become a successful artist. He'd gone out to Arizona in the 1960s as a two-hundred-dollar-a-month cowboy while he learned how to draw and paint. Then he got into real estate and became wealthy, which enabled him to focus on his painting. He ended up living a pretty idyllic life.

Joe was just hitting his stride artistically when, in the spring of 2006, he slipped off his horse while dragging a calf to the branding fire. It was a heart attack, and they say he was dead before he hit the ground. Old Joe lived the classic cowboy rags-to-riches story, and he ended it with the perfect cowboy death.

Beef, Beans and Bullshit finally ran out of gas around the time Joe died. Chas was doing all the organizing but got too overloaded. He went through a hard divorce, and his recent years have been like mine.

In the early 1990s, around the time Beef, Beans and Bullshit began, Adelita started going to Longview School. This really connected us to the Longview community. Before that, as far as local social life went, Twylla and I would go to the bar and that was pretty much it. The only people I knew were the cowboy friends I rode with — the wild bunch. I didn't know any of the farmers and didn't really want to know them. But through Adelita, Twylla and I discovered what a nice little town Longview is. It's a close-knit community, though it has its share of gossip and small-town politics too.

Many of the parents were heavily involved with the elementary school. Rosemary Bews — who was married to bronc rider Tommy Bews, who helped me in the OH Ranch fight — drove the school bus. Twylla and her friend Delilah Miller helped out with all kinds of school projects throughout the year, especially at Christmas and Easter. And I'd play the guitar at Christmas pageants, where Adelita and the other kids would stand onstage forgetting their lines and looking cute.

Longview School was without peer back then. Schools are only as good as their staff, and Adelita benefited from the luck of the draw, attending the school when some good people were working there. Staff members such as Karen Wight and Jim Critchley really got involved in the children's lives. Their dedication and work ethic set the tone for the rest of the school.

Unlike her old man, Adelita did very well scholastically: she is very bright and has a lot of drive. And she didn't excel only at school. She's a born horsewoman, a cowgirl right from the start. A chubby-faced little girl with blond hair, she did everything right — except for putting on her spurs. For some reason she had trouble with that for a while, and it would make her furious. She'd sit on the bed of the truck cursing and swearing and working up a sweat trying to put them on. "You've got 'em upside down," I'd tell her. She would just keep growling and trying to do it herself.

Once I tried putting her on one of our young horses, Randy. It was a stupid thing to do but I really thought he'd be fine. Instead he got offended that this little kid was on him and he started to go back to the barn. Then he began to buck a bit. Adelita grabbed that saddle horn in a death grip. She eventually came off, but she darn near got him rode.

When we had our last big calf branding at the ranch in the mid-1990s, down in the willows east of the stone house, Adelita was riding a little horse called Spinner. I'd bought him in Wyoming from the Miller Ranch. He was a soft-hearted little guy, a real child's horse, and he gave her his whole heart and soul. But at the branding, Spinner got spooked and came apart on her. This time she rode him. Any other person probably would have fallen off, but Adelita hung on as he bucked around. All the cowboys who were there for the branding thought it was great. She was only eight or nine at the time.

In junior high Adelita didn't get into trouble like other kids. She didn't get into fights and she and her buddy Hannah certainly weren't into smoking or drinking. (Hannah still comes by the ranch occasionally and brings me vegetables from her mother's garden. She's a good kid.)

Unfortunately, Adelita didn't like Clay very much when she was younger. She had no reason to dislike him but she'd always say, "He's not my brother."

"He's your half-brother, Adelita," I'd reply.

She's past that now, but back then the idea of having a half-brother in Toronto who was almost twenty years older was too much. Today Clay and Adelita don't see each other. I'd love to get them together at the ranch but I've never been able to orchestrate it. I'm sure they'd get along great if I did.

Twylla and I did everything we could to spoil Adelita rotten as she was growing up, giving her skis, televisions, horse equipment and clothes by the ton. But it just didn't take. She has a strong character. It's not that she doesn't like the finer things in life or doesn't have a well-developed sense of entitlement. She does, but she's very level-headed too.

Adelita started riding the amateur circuit in Alberta while she was in junior high, and she found success pretty quickly. At the Writing-on-Stone Rodeo, when she was twelve or thirteen, she won a beautiful buckle embedded with emeralds. That sort of thing puts stars in a kid's eyes. It also put stars in her mother's eyes — maybe more so than Adelita's.

I had stars in my eyes too. All through the '80s and into the '90s I was doing a lot of cutting contests, trying to balance music and horses and family but ultimately having little success with the balancing act.

The reality is that you can't be the best at everything you do. I've learned that the hard way, and I've tried to tell that to my friend Wylie Gustafson, a Montana western singer who also got snakebit by the cutting bug. "You can't be at the top of your game cutting horses and at the same time be at the top of your game in the entertainment business," I told him. "It can't be done." Something inevitably slides, whether it's the music or the cutting or the marriage. Top cutters show all the time — at least every weekend. How can you do that, play concerts *and* spend time with family?

I tried but I could never find the right balance. I was away from home a lot as Adelita was growing up, and with the horses I couldn't show successfully. My hand would move or something else would go wrong and I'd get disqualified. I went to the Fort Worth futurity numerous times but made the finals only once, in 1989, under the guidance of my friend Bill Glass. Finally I realized that being as good as I was at music had taken me a long, long time — not just years but decades. I wasn't a natural musician, so I had to work very hard to become successful.

With my big ego, it took me a long time to put all this into perspective. I finally resolved that I would get my satisfaction from training a nice horse. There's nothing wrong with that. It's the essence of the cowhorse endeavour: making the horse a willing partner instead of just forcing it to do something. You can make them do it, but that's certainly not the way I want to be with my horses in my declining years.

You've got to take joy in making really good ponies, because the world out there is not fair. The pros have to ride sixteen or even eighteen hours a day to stay competitive. It's an exhausting life. The workload is absolutely crushing, and that's why it's better to be a non-pro like me — I can sell and train horses and compete with the pros if I want to. (The significant distinction between a pro and a non-pro cutter is that a non-pro can't take money for training somebody else's horses.) I realized that I could stay a non-pro and still be reasonably competitive.

In the music world in the early 1990s, I was riding a post-*Cowboyography* wave, doing my best to take western music to the next level by mixing reggae and other forms with cowboy music. A classic example is the song "Jaquima to Freno," off my 1991 record, *And Stood There Amazed*. I really pushed the envelope with that song. Jaquima is bastardized Spanish for a hackamore, a rawhide bridle without a bit that eliminates potential damage to the horse's mouth from a metal bit. The use of the hackamore is a secretive old tradition in the West, and just like the legendary cutters, the old Californio hackamore men would never freely divulge those secrets. They kept their knowledge to themselves.

I based "Jaquima to Freno" on Bob Dylan's "Mr. Tambourine Man" dream fantasy concept. Essentially I had decided to do a cowboy version of Dylan's song, but I made it completely different musically. The lyrics of that song are pure fantasy:

Jaquima to Freno
He's an old vaquero
From another time
Hands as fine as the dealers of Reno

He been to the ocean
He been to the sea
Big long tapaderos hangin' both sides
Of an old Visalia tree

Hey Mr. Vaquero
Put a handle on my pony for me
Teach me the mystery

I knew the folklorists might not approve of the song, but the buckaroos loved it, which meant there was nothing the folklorists could do about it. To this day "Jaquima to Freno" is one of my most requested songs.

I wrote and recorded some of my best work in the 1990s. But as the decade wore on, my record sales slowly declined. Each new album sold fewer copies than the previous one. Nobody stays hot forever, and cowboy singers are no exception.

Eighteen Inches of Rain (1994) was my last record that got regular airplay. The radio stations played the hell out of "Alcohol in the Bloodstream," which is good country rock. My cowboy fans' favourite song, "MC Horses," is also on that record. I wrote it in the little cabin behind my corrals, an old line shack I had brought up from someplace near Chimney Rock. Sam Bush's groove on the mandolin really brought that song home in the studio.

"MC Horses" is about the breakup of the legendary MC Ranch in Oregon, one of the biggest cow outfits in the West. When they sold the MC in the early '90s, somebody sent me a catalogue of everything they were selling, including the horses. It was a sad event for the West. I decided to write the song after I overheard two cowboys talking about the sale in a bar.

> *Yeah the people they come from everywhere*
> *Just to bid on 'em high and low*
> *And thereby own a piece of the legend*
> *With the cowherd all dispersed*
> *The ol' cavvy, she had to go*
> *Back in August — 100 head and more*

After I wrote "MC Horses," I learned a lot about the MC's history from William Kittredge, a grandson of Oscar Kittredge, the man who oversaw the MC. Bill is a former

University of Montana English professor and a fine novelist. He's another of my favourite western writers, and his book *The Willow Field* is a modern classic, even though it has yet to get the recognition it deserves.

I'm fascinated by the story of the MC. Bill Kittredge was raised there, and like everyone else in his family, he thought he was doing God's work on the ranch. But after he left he realized how much environmental degradation his family had caused by adopting industrial-style ranching methods. To get more farmland they'd drained all the swamplands, with terribly disruptive results. "It turned out we had wrecked all we had not left untouched," Kittredge writes in his book *Owning It All*. "The beloved migratory rafts of waterbirds, the green-headed mallards and the redheads and canvasbacks, the cinnamon teal and the great Canadian honkers, were mostly gone along with their swampland habitat." The only holistic aspect of the MC was its buckaroo division, out on the desert moving the cattle the old-time way. Everybody who's anybody in the American West buckarooed at the MC for a time, just as they probably buckarooed at the Spanish Ranch in Nevada.

In my song I describe the sale of the MC horses without passing judgment on how the ranch was run. I've never been preachy in my songwriting. The writers I admire just say what's going down; it's the way they describe it that makes it art. In Michael Ondaatje's *Divisadero*, for example, you can see the evolution of California and agriculture through what happens to the characters in the novel. In the same way I do my best to describe the land, the animals and the people who have made their homes in this beautiful, difficult territory. I'd rather tell a story than preach.

That's one reason (among many others) why I'd be a terrible politician. For some reason, a few of my listeners have thought otherwise. Around the time *Eighteen Inches of Rain* came out in 1994, I received the Order of Canada and they wined and dined me in Ottawa. Soon afterwards, the federal Reform Party started sniffing around, wondering if I'd run for them. A bunch of provincial parties were curious about me as well. I never gave the idea much thought. I knew myself well enough by then to recognize that I'd be the worst politico in the country. I don't have the right chemistry. You have to make big intellectual compromises to go into politics. Plus, I don't suffer fools well. I don't have the patience and I'm not a good schmoozer — two key requirements for a politician.

That's also one of the big problems with my songwriting career. Schmoozing to sell your work is a big aspect of songwriting; that's how you get important covers. I got one big cover in the early 1990s, thanks to Tommy Spurlock, a Fort Worth cowboy musician who played steel guitar for me. He was doing some sessions with country up-and-comer Suzy Bogguss when he said, "Why don't y'all do 'Someday Soon,' that old song of Tyson's?" They all gave him blank looks. Then they got the Judy Collins version of the song and cut it almost exactly the same way, with minor tweaking, for Suzy's album *Aces* — and it became a monster hit. That cover made me a lot of money, probably between two hundred and three hundred thousand dollars. In purely financial terms I think "Someday Soon" has been bigger for me than "Four Strong Winds," but that's not because of any schmoozing on my part. Schmoozing ain't my style. I'd rather be with horses.

A lot of my music comes right from the horses — both my experience with horses and research about horses. I wrote "La Primera," my song about the Spanish mustangs coming to America in 1493, in the stone house, using J. Frank Dobie's *The Mustangs* as well as other sources. It turned out to be one of those *Cowboyography*-type songs that just flowed. There are passages in there that just wrote themselves. I don't know how that works, but sometimes it just happens. (A few years after I wrote the song, I got to visit the Pryor Mountains in Wyoming, where bunches of Spanish-type mustangs still run free.)

What I found fascinating while researching "La Primera" was how the Spanish kept meticulous records on the horses that came over from Spain. They even kept information on fowl and feral hogs. Hidden away in Mexico City museums, the records contain the names of all the horses, including the ones that died on the ships. They were all studs and mares — the Spanish didn't geld their horses. Those were incredible animals, a mixture of Andalusian, Arabian and Barb, bred for beauty and strength. They were tough animals; they had to be, in order to cross the sea and carry the *conquistadores* into battle.

Horses had been indigenous to the Americas before the last ice age, but then they vanished, going the way of the woolly mammoth and the sabre-toothed tiger. By bringing their animals with them on those early voyages, the Spanish returned horses to North America. Eventually a few escaped from their masters, and these *mesteños* — stray animals — proliferated like crazy because the environment was perfect for them. They had returned to their ancestral home, and I believe they knew the land in some unconscious, genetic way.

"La Primera" was on *Lost Herd* (1999), my best album in my opinion. *Lost Herd* is my songwriting at its best. It shouldn't have worked so well, as it was recorded in three different places: Calgary, Nashville and Toronto. I haven't a clue how it came off, and nobody else does either. There was no Adrian Chornowol involved; I produced most of the songs myself, and I'm probably the world's worst record producer. The engineers and studios weren't handpicked and I'd never been to the studio in Nashville before. But the record had a magic nonetheless. Go figure.

I wrote several of the songs for *Lost Herd* in Sonoita, Arizona, where I was looking to rent or buy a place to get away from the Alberta cold. I'd used a network of camps in the American West over the years — I'd stay in a cabin and take care of the place for a few days at a time, keeping the kindling box full — but I wanted my own camp. I had heard of Sonoita through the cowboy underground. Everybody said, "It hasn't been spoiled yet." At the time the place was just a highway crossroads amidst beautiful high-altitude grasslands, several thousand feet above Tucson and the Sonoran Desert floor.

I went down there after Ross Knox, a cowboy poet and friend of mine, put me in touch with Bruce André, foreman at the Vera Earl Ranch near Sonoita, a ranch built in the 1960s by the Beck family from Ohio. After I arrived I checked into the old hotel in Patagonia, just down the road from Sonoita and only seventeen miles from the Mexican border. I met Bruce and liked him right away. He's a big, congenial guy, a kid from the Midwest who had always wanted to be a cowboy, and that's exactly what he became. He also studied engineering, and he built Mrs. Beck a steel corral complex, a marvel of engineering full of precision hinges and spring-loaded gates. Bruce does fine work but he also has a wild attitude. He was like the Alan Young of Sonoita.

The old Arizona brush cowboys were starting to disappear from the area and Sonoita was becoming all yuppied up. Bruce took me around to a lot of places that just weren't for me — vacation houses for rich people from Phoenix, stuff like that. Finally, on the last day I was there, he said, "You know, there's an old homestead inholding in the mountains that goes right back to the Apache days." That caught my attention. "I haven't been up there for a while, but maybe we should take a look."

The place Bruce was referring to was a quarter-section completely surrounded by the Vera Earl Ranch. The building was what they call a territorial. That's the ranch-style house down there, with a veranda that goes all the way around the low-slung building. Part of the house was adobe, and there was a swamp cooler — a refrigerator-like cooling device used in the desert — on the roof. When we arrived, the door was hanging wide open.

Shit, I thought, *this place could be full of rattlesnakes.* That didn't sit well with me, but I wanted the place anyway. It was owned by a schoolteacher, Rene Prentice, whose husband had recently died. I looked her up and cut a deal with her to rent the house, and she showed me where everything was. She was a typical American desert lady.

"Want a gun?" she asked as she showed me around. "There hasn't been any trouble here so far, but you never know."

"Sure," I said. She passed me a loaded .38 and a box of cartridges.

The place was wonderful — real cow country. Perfect for songwriting. To get to the house you had to drive seven miles off the secondary highway up a very rocky trail, so nobody bothered me there. The only person who ever tracked me down was my saddle salesman friend, the peripatetic Blaine McIntyre.

The homestead backed right onto the Santa Rita Mountains and it hadn't been developed at all. I did a lot of hiking there. There was lots to see: wild cattle, the occasional cougar and bunches of javelinas — hoofed little mammals that look like pigs. People said they'd even seen a jaguar there once.

I made some good friends at Sonoita, such as "Cattle Kate" Ladson, who ran the quarter-horse division on the Beck ranch. She was a typical cowgirl — all banged up, with knees that were shot — and she and her girlfriend were always in party mode. Whenever Kate was around, it was Pincher Creek all over again. I was riding well back then, so I helped her a lot with her cutting. She had an old roan stud horse, a real gentleman, that I'd ride and cut on.

A few times Bruce and I went across the Mexican border to Nogales. Back then the border turnstile into Mexico was wide open — you just walked right in. Nogales isn't as bad as Juarez, but it's pretty Wild West. If you want to get yourself shot, that's a real easy place to get it done. But Bruce was something of a fearless outlaw, and a gun-hand too, which helped.

One time we were in a Nogales bar looking for guys who sold riatas (lassos), since they're handmade down there.

All of a sudden the lights went out. "Holy shit, we better get out of here," I said to Bruce. We did, and when we got outside, we looked up and saw a dead Mexican up on the power pole. He had got barbecued trying to steal power; that's what cut the lights. Happens all the time down there, they say.

We decided to cross back into the U.S. The border turnstile was wide open going into Mexico, but it didn't swing the opposite way coming back. We had to deal with the border guard. "Don't tell him you're from Canada, for Christ's sake," Bruce said.

I wasn't keen on that plan, given my history with border agents. "Bruce, if they catch me in a lie, I'm screwed."

We got up to the turnstile and the border guy said in his Texas drawl, "Y'all see that? See that dumb sonofabitch? He fuckin' fried. Where you boys headed?"

"Sonoita," Bruce said.

"Go on through." And that was it — yet another time I got cut slack at the border because I'm a cowboy. They can tell if you're real or not. They look at your hands and your colour. If you have a white forehead and you're dark from the nose down, you're probably a cowboy. If you're a wannabe cowboy, they're never as lenient.

I wouldn't go down to Nogales with Bruce after that, because if they catch you lying, you *are* screwed, like I told him.

Those were good times in Arizona but it was the beginning of the end for Twylla and me. She came to visit me in Sonoita with Adelita once or twice, but she didn't like

Adelita, Twylla and me in Sonoita, Arizona. (COURTESY IAN TYSON)

Cattle Kate or her girlfriend because she figured they were after me.

At the same time I thought she was being overly friendly with Ross Knox. There was a heavy vibe between us. Nobody discussed it, but it was there. By this time Twylla and I weren't sleeping in the same bed, and if we did, nothing was going on.

Both of us are pretty moody, and neither of us was putting the necessary effort into our marriage. Part of the problem was my busy cutting and concert schedule, but I can't blame it all on that. People change and marriages evolve, and that's when you really have to work at it. I don't care who you are — you have to work at marriage day in and day out. You've got to slog it out in the trenches. That can be hard to do, but if you don't put in the effort, the relationship eventually becomes hostile. The sad truth is that Twylla and I both knew full well what was happening, but neither of us did a thing about it.

I wrapped up the decade by playing the millennium bash at Ranchman's. That was a redemptive experience after putting in all those shitty nights there in the 1980s. I hadn't been to the place in years, and this time people were actually listening — not just my fans who came to hear us play but the regulars too. The old gang had finally got it.

In the new year I took Clay on tour with me as an opening act for a few concerts in Ontario. On paper, having Clay Tyson open for Ian Tyson looked great. He'd left Look People by this point and was trying to do his own solo acoustic material, but it wasn't fully realized. To make matters worse, he didn't get along with my players. He was very opinionated back then, and the guys got sick of hearing his take on everything. It made for a rather uncomfortable tour.

Clay put out a CD in 2000, but he hadn't quite matured musically and found his own voice. Eventually he got out of music and became a bicycle courier. Bike couriers have quite a subculture — a real fraternity. "We're the last buckaroos, Dad," he would say. I thought that was a pretty good analogy. Riding a bicycle on the icy winter streets of Toronto is a pretty dangerous lifestyle, just like riding cowhorses. Clay realized he'd get killed if he kept working as a bike courier, so he got out of it a while back. He'd developed an interest in customizing bikes and decided to start up his own bicycle shop in the east end of Toronto. He loves it, and he's done well for himself. When I visit him, I can see that he's much more relaxed than he used to be — a happier person altogether.

I'm so glad that Clay discovered a type of work that he can enjoy. He's a stand-up guy, and his sense of honour makes me proud. Last time I was in his shop, he was playing a Sons of the Pioneers LP. In typical Clay fashion, he was playing it on an old Victrola record player. He loves the old cowboy stuff, and I think he still plays a little for his own amusement. I'd love to be a fly on the wall and hear what he sounds like now. I have no idea what it would be like, but I'll bet he probably sounds like himself.

CHAPTER 10

Raven Rock

I sat by myself in the stone house, alone on the ranch. Spring comes late on the northern plains, and this March morning in 2008 was no exception. The divorce had been finalized in February. It was officially all over between Twylla and me.

Adelita wasn't talking to me either. In breakups like these there has to be a villain and a hero. It simplifies the whole process, gives it a cold logic: this is the good person, this is the bad person. Adelita was firmly in her mom's camp when we split. She seldom wrote or called.

Estranged from my twenty-two-year-old daughter, I played an arpeggio riff on the guitar and started writing lyrics, thinking of the kid and resisting the easy temptation to rhyme.

Poplar trees are turning
How long has it been now
Since I've heard a word from you

Since you blessed me with a smile
How long has it been

My thoughts drifted back to happier times, as often happens with songwriting. I thought of the days when, as a nine-year-old, Adelita would hop off the school bus at the end of the driveway and dash up to the corrals, saddle up Spinner and ask me to ride with her. Back then I was her hero. Together we'd cross the road and race on the west-side hayfield with the Rockies as our backdrop. Spinner always beat Bud, which pissed Bud off no end. We raced again and again on that field. Adelita didn't care about badger holes and neither did I.

How our horses could not wait to run
School bus afternoons in early fall
The races that you always won
Through the fields of our dreams

Happy times, but everything had soured since. Twylla and I had neglected our marriage for years. Finally she said to hell with it and ditched the ranch and me. She decided to take Adelita on the rodeo circuit, pulling the kid out of the Catholic high school in nearby Okotoks where she was a straight-A student. Adelita jumped at the chance to bust off the ranch. She hit the American circuit with her mom and finished the rest of her classes online. They headed south with the dually truck and trailer, camping in friends' yards for months at a time so Adelita could compete.

There's no question that Adelita is a good horsewoman. She's no gunsel; she's always been a natural and she'd had a

Adelita barrel-racing at the Steamboat Springs Pro Rodeo Series in Colorado. (COURTESY IAN TYSON)

lot of success in barrel racing. She was about sixteen when she started running with the pros, but there she had less success. Spinner couldn't quite compete with the pro horses.

Twylla thought the solution was to buy Adelita's way into the big leagues with an expensive horse. I was wary of that plan. I've seen enough oilmen go to futurity cutting-horse sales and pay $160,000 for a horse, then you never hear of them again.

Charmayne James became a world champion barrel racer when she was only fourteen, and she had made her own horse, a fabled animal called Scamper. Charmayne's people were poor feedlot cowboys in Clayton, New Mexico, on the Texas line — about as far out in the sticks as you can get. They came up the hard way. Charmayne *had* to make her own horse. That's what most of the female racers do, and I think that helps them gain a much better perspective on life and their careers.

But Twylla wanted Adelita on the fast track, so I paid $43,000 for a horse. Adelita stepped up in class with the new horse, but she was still getting beat. This kind of thing happens a lot. A kid blows everybody away on the amateur rodeo circuit in Alberta, then she gets stars in her eyes and decides to turn pro, thinking it'll be a cakewalk. That's when she'll often hit a brick wall. The gap between the talented amateur rider and the pros is like the Grand Canyon.

Twylla, meanwhile, was spending a ton of money. While she's capable of being a sensible woman, she really lost it during that period. It might have been a cathartic thing for her, but the spending was really getting out of hand. I did my best to cut off the flow. It had to be done.

For a while Twylla and Adelita were back and forth to the ranch, since Twylla had her bank accounts and credit card bills and everything else here — more than twenty years' worth of her life. (Given that fact, it's pretty amazing how thoroughly she seemed to sever the connection.) I was paying most of the bills, and I guess that enabled her to walk out and come and go as she saw fit. On one of her last trips she left me a note with an ultimatum: she wanted signing authority for my ranching and music companies, though, of course, I'd still be the guy paying for everything. No way, I said.

From there it got ugly, turning into the classic Mexican

standoff, with the lawyers running the show. The whole thing was a wreck. Our union was deemed a "marriage of long standing" under Canadian law, which meant that Twylla would get half of everything in the divorce. She came and took all her stuff and much of our artwork from the house while I was touring. It was a big shock to come through the door and find that a lot of my artifacts were gone.

I was a wealthy man back then, thanks to the hard nego-tiating of my agent, Paul Mascioli. Divorce is supposed to be a fair fifty-fifty split, but it never seems to work out that way. Land prices were soaring when the divorce went down — bad news for me. People were getting seven or eight hundred thousand dollars for a quarter-section out here. The land craziness meant that my spread was evaluated at twice what it's worth now.

Meanwhile, Harris Dvorkin, the owner of Ranchman's who had taken Twylla into his family in the 1970s, poured as much gasoline on the fire as he possibly could, seemed to relish the role of adviser, taking Twylla's side all the way. She also got half of my publishing catalogue, which means she gets half of my songwriting royalties. I couldn't catch a break — that's just how the cards got dealt.

I don't think the high divorce rate in our society has any-thing to do with the emancipation of women or feminism or anything like that. It's due to people being people: males being males and females being females. Simple as that. You can see it in horses. They have trouble living together too. Bud is mean to Pokey but she's devoted to him, even though he'd like to get the feed buckets right together, side by side, so she can't have anything. He's totally selfish. Yet the meaner he gets, the more she loves him. It's crazy.

The divorce was tough. The lawyers made a lot of money. The accountants made a lot of money. Twylla made a lot of money. And I signed all the cheques. As they say at the rodeo, I missed the short go — the championship round — again.

As all of this was going down, four green Mounties were gunned down in the line of duty near Mayerthorpe, Alberta. This happened in March 2005, shortly after Twylla and Adelita had left for good. The killings hit the province like a hard punch in the gut, leaving people sick and dazed. Everybody wondered, How could this have happened? Those rookie officers were so young. The oldest, Constable Leo Johnston, was only thirty-two. The other three — constables Brock Myrol, Peter Schiemann and Anthony Gordon — were in their twenties.

A few days after the killings, an RCMP inspector called me on the ranch phone.

"Would you sing 'Four Strong Winds' at the memorial service?" I've had difficulty with that song off and on over the years. In the Ranchman's days there were times when I'd flat out refuse to play it. I regarded it as a relic of my folk years, representing a place I didn't particularly want to go. But I was more than willing to sing the old song on this occasion. "Just give me directions and I'll be there."

I stopped off for Mel Wilson, one of my old pickers, on Thursday, March 10, and we headed north to Edmonton in my truck. There we rendezvoused with two Mounties at a south-side Tim Hortons. One of them was a woman who had served in Africa for several years. She and her partner drove us to the University of Alberta Butterdome, and as we approached the campus, I was struck by the immensity of what we were about to do. The place was packed with cops from everywhere in Canada and the U.S., people who'd come from as far away as Boston and Texas to pay their respects to the fallen police officers. *I can do this*, I thought to myself.

The political dignitaries read their tributes to the fallen officers. Governor General Adrienne Clarkson expressed it well when she said, "Most of us cannot truly understand what it means to embrace a profession that always holds the possibility of danger or death. We count ourselves blessed, though, that dedicated men and women take on this challenge, sustaining the peace, the order, and the freedom that we cherish."

It seemed that sadness and solidarity were present in equal measure in the Butterdome that day. As I listened to the speeches, I knew my performance of the old song would be emotional. I wanted it to be honest and authentic too. I played the song slowly and mournfully, like a dirge:

> *Four strong winds that blow lonely*
> *Seven seas that run high*
> *All those things that don't change*
> *Come what may*
> *But our good times are all gone*
> *And I'm bound for moving on*
> *I'll look for you if I'm ever back this way*

My guitar pretty much played itself, and as I sang, I felt the music resonate throughout the hall.

Afterwards I shook a few hands, Melvin packed up the guitar and we headed home. I didn't realize at the time that my performance had been televised (I don't remember signing a release). But suddenly the old song was back in the limelight again.

A couple weeks after the memorial, I was riding a colt up in my round pen. It was a cold March day and I had the truck door open with the radio cranked up, tuned in to the CBC. Jian Ghomeshi was counting down the top songs for a series called *50 Tracks: The Canadian Version*. The idea was to let CBC listeners pick the "essential Canadian popular songs" of the past century. "Four Strong Winds" had been nominated for the list. I was curious to see how far it would go, so I listened as he counted 'em down.

"From 1981, 'Northwest Passage,' written and recorded by Stan Rogers — the number four song. . . . At number three, from his groundbreaking record *Harvest,* here's Neil Young and 'Heart of Gold' from 1971."

My song hadn't made the cut. Too bad.

"The second most essential Canadian popular song of the last hundred years: the Barenaked Ladies, and 'If I Had $1,000,000.'"

I could see Lightfoot taking number one. Ghomeshi interviewed music critic Nicholas Jennings before announcing the top song. "If you don't get goose bumps listening to this song, I think your Canadian citizenship should be revoked," Jennings said.

Ghomeshi continued: "This is a song that seems to have had an air of destiny about it from day number one. Ladies and gentlemen, the number one Canadian popular song: Ian & Sylvia, 'Four Strong Winds.'"

I damn nearly fell off my colt. It was surreal. The wind is howling, horse turds are blowing across the pen and I'm riding in circles freezing my ass off — and Jian Ghomeshi announces that a song I wrote in Albert Grossman's New York flat back in 1962 is the top Canadian song of all time. The phone started ringing off the hook with friends calling to pass along their congratulations.

I've been told that after my performance at the RCMP memorial, the number of votes for "Four Strong Winds" in the CBC contest increased dramatically. It's almost as if the old song had been reborn out of tragedy.

And then I lost my voice.

It was the summer of 2006 and I was playing the Havelock Country Jamboree in Ontario, a big outdoor hoser festival about a hundred miles northeast of Toronto. I'd had a bad experience with the sound guys there when I played the festival in 2001. This year I was having even more trouble. It was as if they'd never heard of acoustic instruments or equalized monitors. They had the bass all cranked up, Nashville rock-and-roll style, and the rest was mud. I started shouting into the mic, trying to out-muscle the system — a stupid thing to do. I should have known better.

When I got off the stage, I knew I'd hurt my voice. It wasn't painful but I could feel a constriction when I was talking with Ray Benson of Asleep at the Wheel, the act that followed us. (I believe Ray brought his own mixer to avoid the problems I had encountered.) I felt terrible, because I knew something very bad had happened.

A couple of months later I caught a bad virus on a plane out of Denver, and after that my voice really shut down. I played some shows and tried to do the best I could, but in Eugene, Oregon, I couldn't sing at all. I just rambled on to the audience (the people there were very sympathetic). When I got home, my doctor told me I had to see a specialist in Calgary. The specialist put a TV camera down my throat and found a lot of scarring. He basically told me, "You're screwed." That scared the hell out of me.

For a while I made different attempts at rehabilitation. I worked with a holistic doctor in Fernie, B.C., who used all-natural potions from Belgium. She did a voodoo-type treatment where she hooked me up to a computer; I'd hold on to two copper clamps and the computer would come up with these coloured bars that she then fed back into the computer. The computer analyzed them and said which nutrients I was missing. I did that for about a year and then thought, *This ain't working.* But now I think it *was* working. In any case, it made me healthier.

These days I have a perpetual cold, a constant low-grade condition. It's not the flu, but if you're a singer, it's not fun. I started developing a Tom Waitsian singing method. I had to find a way, and I slowly figured out a technique that worked with my new croaking, gravelly voice. I call it "raven rock." The ravens living near me seem to understand my new voice. They leave in the wintertime and come back in March or April. They lived in my little coulee a few years back and then moved a bit closer, into the rickety poplar trees, before moving right into the hayshed. I was surprised when they settled that near, since they don't usually like to live close to people. But they seem to think I'm one of them. I croak at them and they croak back, even though I don't know what they're saying.

It was all very well that the ravens were fans of my new voice, but I was still unsure about what my fans would think. I didn't know whether I should keep going with music and do another album to follow up *Songs from the Gravel Road,* my 2005 release. *Gravel Road* had been overproduced and it got mixed reviews; many critics resented the jazz mix in there and thought it was out of character. But I liked that album a lot, *especially* the jazz songs.

Music critics tend to have preconceived ideas of what an artist should sound like. They want to put things in little boxes with labels. If you let that limit you as an artist, you're making a big mistake. It's not productive to worry about what the critics will think when you're writing songs. If you're going to be an innovator, you have to innovate, and realistically you can't hit it out of the park every time.

At this stage in the game I'm interested in doing something new, fresh and creative. I like to tell stories and I want those stories to be clothed in interesting music. On *Gravel Road,* for example, I did a song about bronc rider Jerry Ambler, an Alberta boy who got killed in a car accident in Utah in 1958. After he died, his Hamley saddle drifted around the West until champion bareback rider Jim Houston rescued it from obscurity and gave it to bronc rider Cody Bill Smith. Finally the saddle journeyed to the Prorodeo Hall of Fame in Colorado Springs. It's a real cowboy story that I chose to tell from the point of view of the saddle, but I put it to a jazz setting. It might not have been the flavour of the day, but I like how it turned out.

Corb Lund also liked *Gravel Road*. He really got it. I first ran into him in 2002, backstage at an Ian Tyson tribute concert at Jack Singer Concert Hall in Calgary, where he played "MC Horses." Corb is a great big, burly Alberta guy — looks like a football player — and very personable. He used to be a punker with an Edmonton band called the Smalls, but I'd never heard of him in that incarnation. He had heard me, though. His veterinarian dad used to play "MC Horses" over and over after my best-of record, *All the Good 'Uns*, came out in 1996. Corb got hooked on my music shortly afterwards, when he discovered *Old Corrals and Sagebrush*.

In 2003 I found out that he was playing at the Bowness Community Centre in northwest Calgary, and my neighbour Pete Wambeke and I hopped in his truck — it was December, cold as hell — and drove up to see him.

I'd heard about an Elvis-type phenomenon happening at Corb's shows, and sure enough, when we got there the women were twenty deep in front of the stage, just like they'd been for me in Bend, Oregon, fifteen years earlier. There was a lot of energy and excitement in that hall, and Corb was very hospitable to Pete and me. He got us backstage and filled us up with booze and then asked me to get up on stage and sing "MC Horses" with him. I did, and the crowd went nuts. Corb eventually cut "MC Horses" on *The Gift: A Tribute to Ian Tyson*, and he did a great job with it.

The whole experience of seeing Corb live gave me pause, because he was singing western stuff when all that was starting to fade. He's kind of like my successor, although he's much more than that too. He's very western but also very Canadian. It will be interesting to see just how big he gets.

With Corb Lund, Bowness Community Hall, Calgary, 2003.

(© TODD KOROL)

Corb became a good friend in a hard time, when my marriage was dying. He would drop by the ranch pretty regularly on his trips down to see his folks in Taber. We'd go riding or go down to the stone house, where he'd drink beer and I'd drink my wine. We discussed horses, music, American politics — and women, of course — long into the night.

My life was very bleak back then and I was drinking pretty heavily, just trying to tough my way through it. If I had been suicidal, quite frankly that would have been the time to off myself. I credit my supportive friends for pulling me through that darkness. My friends worry about me a lot — probably with good reason — and the ones who live in the area are always calling and getting me out for a meal.

But they also give me my space, because they realize I'm pretty good at being a bachelor. I don't need to be around people all the time — never have — but a man does need human contact, and my friends have made a huge difference in my life in recent years. They're very loyal and understanding. They're there for me.

A new romance also gave me hope during that period. I had fallen in love with a woman who had been coming to my shows all over the West. We starting running together around the same time Twylla and I broke up, although one wasn't the result of the other. I was very much in love with this woman, and the way I imagined it, she would eventually move up to the ranch and we'd live together. We'd meet up at an old ranch house in Colorado. The ranch was still running cattle and horses, so it was a very cool rendezvous spot for us. I lived for the weekends when I could fly to Denver and get with her.

Music also got me through the darkness. If I hadn't had music, I'd be gone. But when I was in the middle of it all, I wasn't sure if I would do another record, given my new voice. Corb, however, was adamant. "Do it," he told me. "I like your new voice better than your old one anyway. Your old voice was getting boring."

He was right about that. My old voice was a good one, but I'd been around too long with it, and I'm not Frank Sinatra. After I got over being terrified about losing my chops, I found that I could draw people in with my new delivery. My croaking made people sit up and listen. I was almost glad it had happened. At concerts I'm telling stories better — because I have to. And the singing comes off well too. When I'm sitting in the stone house in the morning, I often feel as if I can't sing at all. But when the time comes to perform, I'm like an old fire-engine horse off to the fire.

So I took Corb's advice and started writing for *Yellowhead to Yellowstone and Other Love Stories*. There are a lot of end-of-the-trail songs on that record. When I was writing "Estrangement" on that spring morning in 2008 and thinking of Adelita, I wasn't holding anything back; it was pretty heartfelt and powerful. I consider "Estrangement" the best piece of music I've ever written.

> *Now I'm waiting out the flight delays*
> *Waiting for the storm to pass*
> *Waiting for the sky to clear*
> *And I see your face*
> *I don't think I know you*
> *But I know I love you still*

Somehow Adelita ended up in Huntsville, Texas (I don't think I was informed of that fact when she went there). She was attending a farmer school called Sam Houston State University, which struck me as an odd move, akin to having all the scholastic qualifications to go to the University of Calgary but choosing a college in Prince George, B.C., instead. (Usually there's a boy involved in these scenarios, but in this case I didn't know the details.) She eventually transferred to Tarleton State University in Stephenville, Texas, which has a top rodeo team. That's a fine school if you're a cowgirl. Adelita's a Texan now — she even talks like one.

We both happened to be in Colorado at the same time just after I wrote "Estrangement" — me visiting my lady, she visiting her boyfriend's people, who live in the area. We went out for Mexican food together. She was kind of feeling me out, and I was doing the same with her. We didn't have a whole lot to say to each other at that lunch, but at least we'd begun talking.

I guess I hit the wall hardest around my seventy-fifth birthday, in September of that year. My friends Bob and Ali O'Callaghan kindly threw me a big party here at the ranch, put up a big tent and everything. They spent a lot of money on it, and it was a fine, high-class affair. I croaked out a few songs and people danced their brains out. Clay came out from Toronto but Adelita wasn't there. My Colorado lover didn't come up for the party either, which left me feeling empty.

On the day of the party, my guitar player of ten years quit on me, with no notice, over a writing dispute. I had taught him a lot about music and life, and he had this idea that his creativity wasn't being adequately compensated. That left us high and dry. Fortunately my bass player, Gord Maxwell, knew of a musician in the Portland area who was available. Lee Worden is a former Vancouver Island boy, like me, and he turned out to be a great guitar player, one of the best I've had. Thanks to Lee, we kept touring.

When I rode at the Fort Worth futurity a few months later, I didn't know if Adelita would bother to come, even though she lived only an hour and a half away. But every time I rode she was there, which was pretty encouraging. She brought her boyfriend (whose name is also Clay) with her. After my first round we all went out for Mexican food — it always seems to be Mexican food — at Uncle Julio's, along with Bill Riddle, my friend and coach. It was very

Didgereydo
2008 NCHA Futurity

Riding Didgereydo at the 2008 National Cutting Horse Association futurity in Forth Worth, Texas. (NCHA PHOTOS)

pleasant; I could see that she was making a real effort to connect with her dad.

I got a letter from Twylla around this time. She'd taken off for the Bahamas, where she was in a relationship, soon after Adelita went back to school. The letter she sent me was full of regrets; she regretted what had happened, she said, and carried a sadness that remained with her. I was sorry about that, of course, but elated when I read those words, because by this time I thought there was no reason why we couldn't be civil to each other. I sure didn't want to be bitter anymore.

The letter had arrived just as I was realizing that the love affair with my Colorado lady would probably never grow into anything larger. The prospect of our living together was looking less and less likely. But Adelita and I were talking again, and that gave me hope.

CHAPTER 11

Closing the Circle

The ravens have returned. This must be their sixth or seventh spring here at the ranch, and the male, jet black, is almost the size of an eagle. When I went to move bales in the hayshed yesterday, I heard the faint mutterings of their babies in the nest, high in the rafters.

Ravens are terrible nest builders, so a few years back I asked my old ranch caretaker, Norman Ring, to install a plywood platform for them. Being an old-fashioned rural Albertan, he thought I was nuts. He was raised to shoot ravens, not build platforms for them. But I like having 'em around, even though they can be noisy as hell.

To the west the coyotes are yipping up on the ridge. Past the ridge, in the mountains, the glaciers are slowly disappearing, but when the plains run out of water, the coyote will survive us all and move on. I'm told they have proliferated well into the east. Perhaps they have grown tired of the diminished West, figuring it's time to leave the countryside and become urbanized. (Carrying this idea of a coyote

In my round pen, on Purple Pop. (SHANNON LAWLOR)

diaspora to absurdity, one can imagine them preying on the chicken coops and vegetable gardens that are springing up in Detroit and Brooklyn.)

Old cowboys have always lamented the West's passing, and I'm no different. The West I fell in love with — herdsmen on horseback riding the open range — is all but gone. There are a few isolated pockets in Alberta where it still exists, but not many. It will likely survive in the real hardcore desert country — New Mexico and northern Nevada — so long as extractive industries don't destroy the land the way they're doing here in Alberta.

It's a tricky paradox: for years I've done my harangue on the disappearing West, but people have been claiming they're witnessing the last days of the West for almost 150 years. Montana photographer L.A. Huffman saw the end way back in 1870 when he visited Yellowstone-Bighorn country, "unpenned of wire." To Huffman, the railroad was the death blow: "There was no more West after that. It was a dream and a forgetting, a chapter forever closed." Then Charlie Russell saw the last of the old West in the 1880s. My old man saw the last of the old West in the 1900s. Ian Tyson and Kurt Markus saw the last of the old West in the 1980s, a full century after Charlie. And Corb Lund is seeing the last of the West today.

The West constantly reinvents itself, like an organism that keeps dying out and being reborn in some new form. Who knows, maybe the grass-finished-beef trend will kick-start cowboying again in certain areas.

Just because my West is compromised doesn't mean that's true for everybody. People from Manitoba and Ontario probably come to Alberta today and think, *This is the real West.* They fall in love with the open spaces and the Rockies, just as I did in the 1970s. Or maybe they get drunk watching the bronc riders at the Calgary Stampede in July and think they've discovered the real West there. I may not agree, but the West has always been in the eye of the beholder.

These days I don't find anything particularly romantic about the modern rodeo or chuckwagon racing. For me the romance of the West is the Rockies. Simple as that. If you took away the Rockies, I'd basically be living in Saskatchewan shooting gophers — and there's nothing romantic about that, no matter how you define it. The Rockies, on the other hand, are so aesthetically over the top — changing every morning, orchestrated by the light — I never get tired of 'em.

These Hutterite ladies are serenading me with "Someday Soon."
(BARRY FERGUSON)

My life sure ain't all beer and skittles, as my old man used to say, but I'm hanging in there. I'm still heading out on the road, still selling out concert halls after fifty years in the business. That's my salvation. The fact that I can still move people with my stories — I live for that. I get a couple of hours of real bliss on stage — until the pain in my hands gets bad. Old age is not for wimps.

When I look back on my life, I can honestly say there's not a hell of a lot I would change. I've certainly had my share of failures, but life is a series of mistakes and correc- tions. The best you can do is honour the truth. That sounds

real easy, but somehow it isn't. We all have different inter-
pretations of the truth and we all mould the truth to suit
our needs. It's part of the human condition. Go back to
Will Shakespeare and it's all there. In the end, you've got
to be honest and truthful, because that's all your fellow
travellers have to gauge you by on the long trail. It all goes
back to the lessons I learned as a bandleader and as a horse
trainer: consistency is of paramount importance. There's
no room for anything less.

But inevitably we all make mistakes. You're going to
wipe out and hit the ditch. It would be a cop-out for me to
blame my indiscretions on the music business or the cowboy
way of life. In the end you just have to hope that the lives of
the people you're closely connected with — family and
friends — will turn out okay down the line. You just hope
that everybody closes the circle, that everybody rides home
the best way they can. Only the wind is forever.

IAN TYSON was one of North America's most respected singer-songwriters. A pioneer who began his career in the folk boom of the 1960s, he was one of the first Canadians to break into the American popular music market. In the years that followed, he hosted his own TV show and recorded some of the best folk and western albums ever made. Tyson was a recipient of the Order of Canada, and received multiple Juno and Canadian Country Music awards. He toured consistently across Canada and throughout the United States, and until his death in December 2022, he continued to live and work on his ranch in the foothills of Alberta's Rocky Mountains.

JEREMY KLASZUS is a Calgary writer and the winner of two National Magazine awards. A former resident of the Banff Centre's literary journalism program, Klaszus has written for *Reader's Digest*, the *Calgary Herald*, *Fast Forward Weekly* and *Alberta Views* magazine. He is the founder and editor-in-chief of *The Sprawl*.